SO MANY WORLDS

Maria Eugenia Haya. In the Lyceum. Havana 1981

SO MANY WORLDS

A Photographic Record of Our Time

Dieter Bachmann and Daniel Schwartz
With a Foreword by Claudio Magris

A BULFINCH PRESS BOOK
LITTLE, BROWN AND COMPANY
Boston • New York • Toronto • London

Acknowledgments

This publication accompanies the touring exhibition *Der
Geduldige Planet. Eine Weltgeschichte in 255 Fotos:* du *1941
bis 1995* (The Patient Planet. A World History in 255 Photos:
du 1941 to 1995), which opened in September 1995 in
Holderbank, Aargau, Switzerland. The exhibition was sponsored
by Pro Helvetia, Arts Council of Switzerland, Zurich.

    The authors wish to thank Nathalie and I-Jong Juan,
Photographers International, Taipei, Taiwan, for their early
support; Holderbank Management and Consulting AG,
Holderbank, Switzerland; Leica International, St. Gallen,
Switzerland; and *Tages-Anzeiger,* Zurich, Switzerland.

Conceived by Dieter Bachmann and Daniel Schwartz
Picture selection made with the assistance of René Burri

Book design by Adam Hay, London

First North American Edition

ISBN 0-8212-2324-0
Library of Congress Catalog Card Number 96-76457

Bulfinch Press is an imprint and trademark of
Little, Brown and Company (Inc.)
Published simultaneously in Canada by
Little, Brown & Company (Canada) Limited

PRINTED IN GERMANY

Contents

Foreword: Claudio Magris
The Patient Planet

The works Havel wrote while under persecution make a case for life versus ideology and persistently seek to distinguish truth from appearance, which every totalitarian regime strives to crush and confound. In one of his essays he recounts how while watching the television one evening, he observed a sudden confused expression appear on the weather forecaster's face when a technical fault interrupted the programme. Havel describes the presenter's face and notes the difference between her original rigid and stereotyped expression and her subsequent disturbed and sincere expression, which restored her spontaneity and revealed her true face.

Havel emphasized the difference between being and performing, between life and spectacle, differences which totalitarian regimes attempt to cancel out. At that time he opposed Brezhnevian communism, but also questioned whether that tyranny might not be 'the caricature of contemporary life in general', and if the situation in Czechoslovakia were not 'in reality a reminder to the West that points out its latent destiny'.

The century – indeed the millennium – that is drawing to a close appears to reveal with brutal clarity the destiny of the planet that Havel perceived brewing in the shadows. Life seems ever more indistinguishable from its representation, and in the world's great performance it is ever more common to feel that one is not just an interchangeable walk-on part, but rather a stand-in for oneself, a silhouette of real life. Once, when I was looking for some books in a library, a librarian asked me, 'Who do you represent?', obviously unable to understand that someone might be himself and want something for himself. Reality appears to be increasingly made up of actions that run parallel to other equally non-existent actions. Only when the smooth organization of the world breaks down do faces appear to regain their truth.

Many of the photographs collected in this book seem to be snapshots that capture moments when an existential truth (with all its yearning for redemption) lights up anonymous faces clouded by the pain of living. The collection opens with a Prologue dedicated to three faces. It is not important whose faces they are, whether they are famous or unknown; the only important thing is that the three archangels who introduce the tragedy and its many acts are three human faces.

A child once said to Biagio Marin, as the old poet stood on the seashore in Grado photographing the sunset, that you should photograph people, not clouds. It can be said that an era is made up of the human faces that have lived through it; these are its identity card which it will have to display when the trumpets sound in the valley of Jehoshaphat. Despite being undermined by psychology and psychoanalysis, often justifiably vituperated physiognomy is given new credence in the era of photography and video; one only need think of the incredible faces so often to be seen on the television for the greater glory of the audience. The soul, according to Marcus Aurelius, is coloured by one's own dreams and thoughts; it is our 'gods' which mould our features. The values a person cherishes are engraved in the lines of his face and shape his expression, becoming his way of being, his gaze, his attitudes and gestures; they reveal his nobility or coarseness, his arrogance, fragility or satisfaction.

From a certain age onwards, we are all responsible for our own faces, which reveal the god or idol to which we make sacrifices in our hearts. The human face does not only bear the wrinkles of our age and the scars of our life, but also the signs etched by the power of our epoch. A frightened, disfigured or worn out face is also an accusation against the world in which it has lived and against those who inflicted those wounds or allowed them to be inflicted. The woman crossing a street, in a photograph by René Burri (p. 53), has a beautiful, drawn face; her mouth, stretched by a tension that cancels out any hint of a kiss, reveals how much she must have lost along the way, perhaps even the ability to be charmed or to be carried away.

There are famous faces, Pound and Picasso, Camus or Cocteau, as well as people I have known: Ingeborg Bachmann, Max Frisch, Uwe Johnson. The last time I saw Johnson was in Trieste, where he was holding a conference entitled 'Brauchen wir einen Roman?' (Do we need a novel?), and he asked me for names of Trieste suburbs and tram lines that he could quote. Do we need a novel? Who knows. Perhaps, after all and in spite of everything, we do.

These photographs can also be seen as a novel, an epic of disillusion and the triumph of temporality; they constitute a journey through obscurity similar to that which surrounds Manhattan (Emil Schulthess, p. 154). The photographs span more than fifty years, half of a century that has been terrible and magnificent, and has not only radically transformed the world but has also seen the individual engaged in a kind of anthropological mutation, the next stage of which and whose final point of arrival cannot be glimpsed. This collection is a history in figures: it reveals an epoch in the concrete form of unrepeatable moments, in a detail, a gesture, a begging hand, a city destroyed by bombs, a dead body. A sequence of separate images is perhaps a fitting way to narrate the fragmented and heterogenous nature of reality, which is increasingly similar to the 'anarchy of atoms' that Nietzsche, and later Musil, believed dissolved every unity, including the unity of the individual ego. Each of the images is separate, unrelated; their kaleidoscope implies that any harmonious totality in the world has been shattered, leaving splinters and chips to rove like flotsam and jetsam bobbing with the tide.

The empty spaces between one photograph and another and the sharp pairings echo the disconnectedness of reality. It is the foreword writer's task to fill the voids, establish links and meanings, and to reassure the reader that all is well, that the image of the world holds and therefore the world also. However, the smooth, full prose of rhetorical consolation cannot soften the effect of the sharp profiles of bony women and children fleeing from Chad across the desert (Masanori Kobayashi, p. 225) or, to take another example, of the skeletal bodies of Greek children suffering from malnutrition (Anon., p. 20), or of the angular corpse of a soldier in Spain (Robert Capa, p. 21). The photo-graphs are not there to be discussed, but to be looked at, and even the scream from a mouth twisted in grief should be heard.

This book portrays an epoch where reality is disconnected, where there is a lack of meaning yet also the nostalgia for a meaning, which flares up suddenly only to die away immediately. The differences between reality and performance vindicated by Havel and denied in totalitarian regimes are corroded in the West, in a process where life is absorbed by its spectacularization. In order for the differences to exist there is a need for a strong ego, individuals with their own tablets of the law and the ability to judge the world. The two great haruspexes of the crises of the modern world, Nietzsche and Dostoevsky, revealed how precarious and weak the individual ego and conscience are. The dissolution of the individual marks the advent of nihilism, against which Dostoevsky struggled, considering it an illness to be overcome, and which Nietzsche, perhaps against his aching sensitivity, forced himself to celebrate as a liberation.

Nietzsche celebrates the 'Übermensch' ('superman'), not an individual with greater traditional qualities, but a new kind of man, a new anthropological stage, a new form of organization of the psychic nuclei, of the 'anarchy of atoms' that make up the seemingly unitary being. This fluid and plural ego dissolves in the flux of life; for him there can be no difference between truth and fiction, since every deep and authentic reality of the person is negated and appears to be entirely made up of the play of its masks and representations. The world today, with its global spectacularization and Dionysian totality that embraces and dissolves the whole of life, perfectly realizes the nihilism foretold by Nietzsche and at the same time cancels out the distinction between true and false, between being and seeming that Havel defended humanistically. This process is in the main a characteristic of the West; however, with the spread of Western lifestyle throughout the world, it is infecting the rest of the planet.

The faces portrayed in these photographs very often reveal a resistance to this process, a tenacious individuality that can be seen, for example, in the strong faces of the Palestinians photographed by Lerski (pp. 121, 124–25). Individuality can be discerned above all in people weighed down by suffering, by the horrors of desperate situations, such as the Warsaw ghetto (Anon., p. 23) and contemporary life. Pained expressions are often accompanied by an irrepressible dignity, which illustrates Isaiah's belief that the Lord chooses the imperfect stone discarded by masons to be the corner stone of His house.

Dignity is to be found in the beaten, in those who are crushed by the violence and absurdity of life and history. The faces of patients in mental hospitals and psychiatric clinics (Carla Cerati, Paul Senn, pp. 227, 230) and in reformatories (Ernst Scheidegger, p. 229) show an extreme, incoercible dignity, the ineradicable mark of suffering humanity. At times it is even objects, such as the Gulag prisoners' boots, thrown randomly on the floor (Thomasz Kizny, p. 94), that express, in the extremes of misery to which man can be subjected, the dignity of grief, the grandeur of the defeated. In comparison with the defeated, or even with the mute suffering of animals, the self-confidence of the victorious, or of those who for an instant delude themselves that they are, is ridiculous and renders each of them, in Manès Sperber's words, a 'cocu de la victoire' (cuckold of victory). The fitting destiny of every millenary Reich is as the débris swept up by the Berlin 'Trümmerfrauen' (Werner Bischof, p. 49), whose brooms clear away the remains of the basest power in history.

It is at times difficult to believe that some of the bestial faces were created in the image and likeness of God. However the photograph of a beggar in Transylvania (Werner Bischof, pp. 96–97) has the power to make one believe once more. The ragged beggar is crouching on the ground, his face is hollow and his thin hair looks as if it has been pulled out. Of the people passing him, only the skirts, boots and suits can be seen; only he has a face. This image comes from the East, from what was called 'the other Europe', which was ignored, feared and contemptuously considered by the West to be a promiscuous dark world; it is now pushing at the doors of the West with a mass of wretched, disadvantaged souls. The Prince of Metternich used to say derogatively that the Balkans began beyond the Rennweg, the main thoroughfare across Vienna, whereas today in Ulm, many kilometres to the west of Vienna, people say that the Balkans (the term once again used disparagingly) begin in Neu-Ulm, on the other side of the Danube. However, the beggar is indomitable, he cannot be assailed by insults and opinions; he is a King in disguise or perhaps one of the thirty-six just men who, according to Jewish belief, stop the world from collapsing. In any case, he is someone. Pirandello stated that a beggar is never banal.

After the Prologue, a photograph of elderly gentlemen sleeping (Salomon, p. 25) appears in the next sections. The caption reads 'Congress sleeps'. It is a timeless photograph, or alternatively it can be described as enveloped in the suspended, stretched time of sleep. The gentlemen are in evening dress, sprawled on a sofa and armchairs in front of a small table with champagne glasses on it; the photograph could have been taken today or many years ago, at the beginning of the century. Sleep is undoubtedly a good thing; Stevenson recounts that the greeting used by the natives of the South Seas was 'sleep and long life'. Sleep is letting oneself go, harmony: the sleep after love described by Isaac Bashevis Singer, the desired sleep of Thomas Mann's Tonio Kröger. The ill of the epoch is insomnia, as Kafka knew well. He described it as a fault, a lack of *pietas*, an inability to let oneself go. The sleep of reason generates monsters, but reason incapable of sleep or of letting go generates fevered and enforced delirium.

There can be odd surprises upon waking. Perhaps the gentlemen dozed off in the summer of 1914, after Sarajevo, when the war had not yet broken out. As in a fairy-tale, they sleep for nearly one hundred years and when they awake they do not realize how much time has passed, because everything is as it was, despite two world wars, the massacres of millions, monstrous totalitarian regimes. The hatred and national wars of that time are blazing – still and once again – past problems are returning, regurgitations belched forth by history. The frozen tensions and conflicts are thawing out in blood baths – Sarajevo, still or once again, is the world's tragic nerve centre.

Children? The section's title should have a question mark, indeed a question mark that would provide the real title. The majority of the children betray no trace of happiness; the freedom and happy smiles of childhood are missing. Only one Burmese child, although carrying a load on his shoulders that makes him appear crucified, shows a timid yet frank smile (Daniel Schwartz, p. 224). Childhood has a majesty that brings it in some respects close to old age. The child is not yet involved, the old are no longer, in the fierce, obtuse mêlée of existence; the child, like the elderly, can evade the principle of reality to a greater degree. Although materially more at the mercy of the world than adults, in their thoughts and imagination children are less conditioned. Social hierarchies have no power over children, something that confers on them a self-sufficiency that can be seen in their gestures, races and games: it is here that their charm lies.

Children should not be idealized; they are not only exposed to the violence of adults but are also incapable of distinguishing good from evil and thus capable of indifference and cruelty, not to mention the affectedness they learn from adults. However, children *are*, independently of any social role; it is this that likens them to some old people, as intimately autonomous as a tree that has no need to be admired and is not worried by a dog cocking his leg on its trunk. There is increasingly less space for children in the world; the population of European cities is ageing, schools and kindergartens are closing, restaurants are more tolerant of dogs than children, a screaming baby is more distressful than a radio at full volume, the starving and afflicted children of the Third World suffer indescribable torments. If all suffering is an outrage, the suffering of children is an unacceptable scandal, a stain on life – Dostoevsky writes that even if it were the price of eternal beatitude, the only correct thing to do would be to refuse it and return the ticket to God. The photograph of starving Greek children (Swiss Red Cross, p. 20) is the ideal centre of the book, an atrocity around which all the rest emptily rotates.

There is little space for childhood in the world since it is the living symbol pointing to that which the world is increasingly losing: the present. The present means life, the moment lived for itself, without being sacrificed for the future, without being nullified in projects and schemes, without being considered merely a moment to be lived through swiftly in order to reach something else. It is almost always the case that we have too many reasons to hope that our existence will pass as rapidly as possible, that the present swiftly becomes the future, that tomorrow comes as quickly as possible, because we are anxiously waiting for the results from the doctor or the outcome of an examination, the beginning of the holidays, the result of an action, and thus we exist not to live but to have already lived, to be closer to death.

Contemporary life has accelerated this process of destroying the present, it propels us ever faster into the future, burning up the present in plans and schemes that spring up everywhere. Childhood is the possession of the present and provides a reproof to adults who have lost it. As a child St Louis of Gonzaga was playing when asked by a relative, with the hypocritical, serious overbearance of the adult, what he would do if he knew he was to die in ten minutes. I would carry on playing, replied the child.

Ruins. A photograph shows Dresden after its destruction by bombs (Walter Hahn, pp. 28–29). The remains of buildings jut upwards into empty space. The destruction provides austere scenery, it denudes reality of any show, it reduces it to its bare essence. Even in Dresden today one comes across the empty spaces left by the carpet bombing of February 13 1945. It would be a good idea not to restore the Frauenkirche, as has, however, been planned; the ruins rise up amid the scattered rubble like a disembowelled body or a face with empty eye sockets. It looks as if it were bombed yesterday and the first rescue teams have just arrived. The horror of war and the madness that engendered it is visible, palpable.

It would be better not to restore it and to leave that eloquent void as a warning against violence. For some time there has been another, invisible and impalpable void surrounding us – a social and cultural vacuum as far as history, political vision and tablets of law are concerned. It is as if the war and the horror have been forgotten and can no longer teach anything, as if everything could be repeated. Until recently it seemed as if antifascism was imprinted on the genetic code of civilization, that Nazism was the definitive face of evil. It now appears that this historic and moral lesson has been weakened: Europe is beset by evils that we thought had disappeared forever, national wars that a short time ago appeared impossible are flaring up again, opinions about Fascism waver and mist over, helped by cultural fashions and dubious persuaders. A famous quotation by Brecht is apt here: the womb that bore those monsters may still be fertile.

In the photograph of Dresden a large black figure, the angel of destruction, looks down on the rubble from the top of a building. Black is still the predominant colour. Pollution, time and weather have darkened the statues decorating façades and domes: black angels, black putti and nymphs, black faces. Life is oxidization and every splendour that adorns and exalts it underlines above all else its friability, celebrates death.

Another empty scene shows the area and warehouses of Trieste's port (Gabriele Basilico, p. 83). Lack and absence characterize this

Adriatic city that was once Central Europe's prosperous and vital outlet to the sea. The great Trieste literature sprang up when the city's politico-economic role was coming to an end; a literary school that was strong on declines sprang from a sunset mistaken for a sunrise. A city of frontiers, of flights. Italian refugees, who in the climate of hate and fierce vendettas after the war, had fled Istria (annexed by former Yugoslavia) losing everything, including their roots, remained camped out in the warehouses shown in the photograph for many years. For these exiles they were years of solitude, poverty, incomprehension and resentment. In her *Verde acqua* Marisa Madieri gives an indelible portrait of that purgatorial situation, of that frontier tragedy.

As three thousand Italians fled from former Yugoslavia, approximately two thousand Italian labourers from Monfalcone near Trieste, militant communists who had experienced fascist prisons and German concentration camps, went to former Yugoslavia to work in a communist country and contribute to the building of communism. A short time later, when Tito broke away from the Soviet Union in 1948, they protested on behalf of Stalin, who for them signified revolution, and were subsequently deported by Tito's regime to two Gulags in the upper Adriatic. They were horribly persecuted yet resisted on behalf of Stalin, who, had he been able, would have transformed the whole world into a Gulag to imprison courageous people such as these.

Frontiers, exile, the lack of a future. As a child, the frontier a few kilometres from my house in Trieste was the frontier that divided the world, the Iron Curtain. Invisible boundaries also divided the city itself, separating its parts; the future of the city was unclear and at times it seemed to have no future but to be a no man's land between one road block and another, between West and East.

'And Trieste, ah Trieste ate my liver.' Joyce, who is shown getting out of a taxi in Paris outside the bookshop Shakespeare and Company (Gisèle Freund, p. 61), saw Trieste as a place of exile that suited his nature. For Joyce the city, like Ireland, gnawed at the liver; it was an unbearable yet fascinating Oedipal womb, which gave rise to promises of happiness only to shatter them immediately; an anachronism where there was everything and nothing, a cul de sac where the threads of history were entangled. He lived very close to where I lived and where I still live; the inns where he was so often drunk in the evenings are as welcoming and picaresque as they were, pleasant resting places for travellers, where one can talk – as the Irish writer did – in the Trieste dialect, a historical, ventriloquial mumbling. There is a plaque on the house where Joyce wrote *Ulysses*, perhaps the last traditional classic epic of universal literature, that sets out the values of a centuries-old tradition, the sacral character of flesh and its withering, of wedlock and procreation, of the home and family to which the wandering man returns in the evening. Leopold Bloom is the patient man, just as the earth is a patient planet.

Patience is born of suffering and reveals, as was taught by the Catholic theologians well known to Joyce, both the conviction of being exposed to an inscrutable necessity and the continual expectation of liberation from its weight, which is so oppressing for each individual and the world, and therefore the expectation of salvation for both. We do not know how long the planet will continue to be patient with us. It could tire and justly begin railing like Faust, 'Und Fluch vor allem der Geduld!' (And the curse of patience, above all!)

Claudio Magris

PROLOGUE

Three faces. Two world-famous, one unknown. Three women, one from Switzerland, one from Italy and one from the USA. Visages (like crossword clues) contain ages… When we look into eyes, eyes look at us. For the Greeks it was Atlas who carried the world on his shoulders: who carries it for us?

Edward Steichen. Gloria Swanson. New York 1924

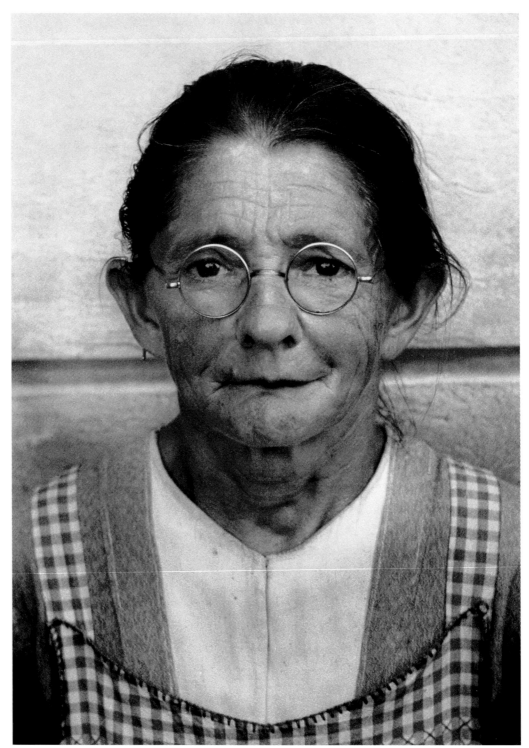

Jakob Tuggener. Textile factory worker. Switzerland 1942

Herbert List. Anna Magnani. Rome 1950

THERE IS A WAR ON

War's shadow was cast early. The rise of Hitler, the persecution of the Jews, Munich, Kristallnacht… By the end of the Second World War 6 million Jews had been killed. And altogether 30 million people died, perhaps many more. All Europe lay in confusion, Germany in ruins. One of the last Allied aerial bombardments was on Dresden – 60,000 dead, 12,000 buildings destroyed. In December 1957, shortly after receiving the Nobel Prize for Literature, Albert Camus said: 'For the artist, no executioner has special rights. That is why today, especially today, beauty cannot be in the service of any party; whether its effect is momentary or lasting, beauty can only serve human pain or freedom.'

Anon. Children watching air raid over London, 1940–41

Anon. Official beginning of the general boycott of Jewish businesses in Germany, 10 o'clock, 1 April 1933

Herbert List. Veiled statue at the German stand at the World Exhibition. Paris 1937

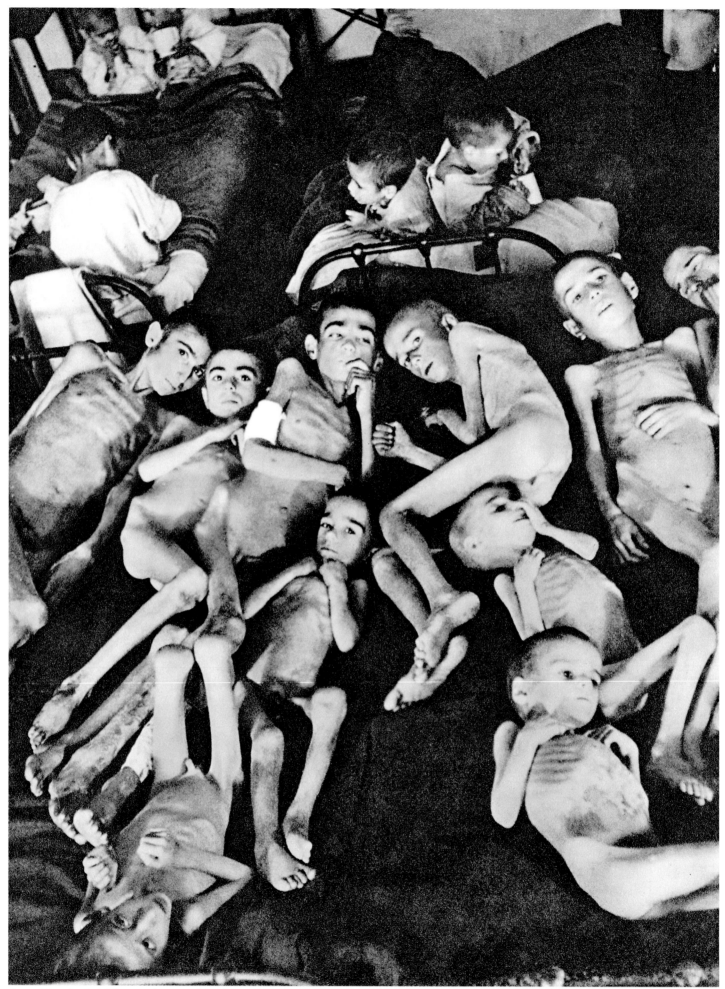

Anon. Deprived children, as discovered by the Red Cross. Greece 1941–42

Robert Capa. Spanish Civil War, 1937

Cas Oorthuys. Starved boy on the way to hospital. Amsterdam during the winter famine of 1944–45

Unknown German army employee. 'Brought out of the bunkers by force.'
Jewish uprising in the Warsaw ghetto, 19 April to 16 May 1943

Mit Gewalt aus Bunkern hervorgeholt. —

René Saint-Paul. Albert Camus, Jacques Baumel and André Malraux at the resistance newspaper *Combat*. Paris 1944

Erich Salomon. First Hague Conference at one o'clock in the morning: Congress sleeps. The Hague, Holland 1929

Anon. German aeroplane crash in a field. England 1941
Following pages: Walter Hahn. Ruins of Dresden seen from the tower of the Town Hall. Germany 1945

Anon. Fleeing from the besieged town of s'Hertogenbosch. Holland, October 1944

SWITZERLAND

Switzerland in the war – an island of special relationships. 'National defence' was something in the mind: keeping the little concerns of everyday life intact, while outside old Europe was sinking. An island which remains neutral; yet not immune from the weaknesses of Hitler's Germany. A patch in the heart of Europe – but also with a heart for Europe? Arnold Kübler, the first editor-in-chief of *du* magazine, from which these pictures come, says in the foreword of the first issue in March 1941: 'Every day calls out to us: You are not alone! You are not just here for your own sake. You have responsibilities and duties beyond those of your own personal inclinations and disinclinations. That is what our title *du* is all about.'

Gotthard Schuh. Awaiting guests. Switzerland, early 1940s

Hans Staub. Breakdown. Switzerland, about 1935

Gotthard Schuh. Women's Auxiliary on active service. Switzerland, early 1940s

Gotthard Schuh. Family on a mobilization day. Switzerland 1939

Jakob Tuggener. Children in the peat diggings. Brüttelen, Switzerland 1944

Anon. Swiss cross being painted as protection against misdirected Allied bombardment on the border with Germany. Boncourt, Jura 1944–45

Ernst Brunner. Allemanda: ring dance on milk day (when farmers meet to declare the milk yield of the previous year) in Guarda, Unterengadin. Switzerland 1939

Anon. Councillors Ette and Celio at the Feast of the canonization of Niklaus von Flüe. Flüeli-Ranft, Switzerland 1947

Paul Senn. Polling day in Wallis. St-Germain, Saviese, Switzerland 1934

Jakob Tuggener. Press ball at the Baur au Lac Hotel, Zurich 1949

Paul Senn. Pablo Casals plays 'Cant des Oscells' as an encore at the Casino, Bern 1941

Jakob Tuggener. At a country inn, Aargau. Oeschgen, Switzerland 1942

Hans Staub. German soldiers, customs officials, police and civilians seeking shelter from the SS in Switzerland. At the Swiss–German border, Basle 1944

WHEN THE WAR WAS OVER

At the end of the war its victims are everywhere. A young Swiss photographer, Werner Bischof, gets his break as a reporter. Germany is divided into two states, Europe into two halves. The Iron Curtain comes down. Directly after the war, an emptiness, a stillness. Clearing up. Hundreds of thousands are still in captivity. But everywhere, wherever there is home, something new is starting: a country is being rebuilt.

Werner Bischof. Hospital train with Italians returning from German camps arriving at Merano. Italy 1945

Werner Bischof. Children's train of the Swiss Red Cross. Budapest 1947

Werner Bischof. Child at play in Maastricht. Holland, autumn 1945

Ruth Berlau. Max Frisch (right) with Bertolt Brecht on the site of
Letzigraben swimming baths, designed by Frisch. Zurich 1948

Werner Bischof. *Trümmerfrauen:* women clearing up bomb sites. Berlin 1946

GERMANY

Germany will never again be what it was. There is the expression *Vergangenheitsbewältigung,* 'coping with the past'; there is the mourning and the shame; there is also suppression. The writers of the 47 Group speak of *Kahlschlagliteratur,* 'demolition literature', and a radical new start. In the West in 1949 the Federal Republic establishes a new rule of law. And in the East, in the same year, the USSR founds the German Democratic Republic. In the West Adenauer ties the Federal Republic to the Western powers. Economic miracle! In 1955, the Federal Republic, with its entry into the Western European Union and NATO, has an army again.

Martin Hesse. Hermann Hesse. Montagnola, Switzerland 1952

René Burri. Retired general on an army manoeuvre on Lüneburg heath. Germany 1959

René Burri. In the garrison town of Baumholder. Germany 1959

Herbert List. Poet Ingeborg Bachmann. Berlin 1959

Herbert List. Helene Weigl, actress and widow of Bertolt Brecht, at a meeting of stage directors. Berlin 1966

René Burri. Writer Uwe Johnson. Zurich 1962

René Burri. German armed forces orchestra on the occasion of General Eisenhower's visit. Bonn 1959

FRANCE

In August 1944 Paris was liberated from the German occupation. The capital of France was spared destruction. Before the war, Paris had drawn writers like Joyce and Hemingway to itself. Now it resumed continuity, experiencing a blossoming of intellectual life that lasted for decades: it was a centre of modern art, with Jean-Paul Sartre and Albert Camus showcasing 'existential literature'; and it was still the favourite destination for world-class authors. Art, literature, fashion, film – Paris was and is the supremely cosmopolitan city once more.

Paul Senn. US sightseers outside a bar. Paris 1945

Gisèle Freund. Resurfacing work on the boulevard Saint-Germain. Paris 1932

Emil Schulthess. Rue Jean Nicot. Paris 1947

Gisèle Freund. James Joyce at the bookshop Shakespeare and Company on rue de l'Odéon. Paris 1938

Lucien Aigner. Break at rehearsal. Paris Opéra 1932

Henri Cartier-Bresson. Pierre Bonnard, Le Cannet. France 1944

Brassaï. Pablo Picasso in his atelier on rue des Grands-Augustins. Paris 1939

Florent Fels. Jean Cocteau. 1937

Henri Cartier-Bresson. Colette with her housekeeper. 1952

Henri Cartier-Bresson. Albert Camus. 1946

Henri Cartier-Bresson. Jean-Paul Sartre. 1946

Henri Cartier-Bresson. Henri Matisse, Vence. France 1944

René Burri. Le Corbusier. 35, rue de Sèvres. Paris 1959

Henri Cartier-Bresson. Georges Braque. 1944

ITALY

Italy is backward. Italy is forward-looking. Italy is a contradiction: between old cities and open fields, between North and South, between industrial and agricultural economies. Italy is conservative-Catholic, with at its heart the state within a state, the Vatican – and Italy is a modern European centre of industry: with the help of the Marshall Plan it is reconstructing its entire economy, society and agrarian system. With 'Neorealismo' it experiences a flowering of film and literature, and remains, despite changing governments, a stable European partner.

Walter Studer. Saying goodbye on the emigration ship MS Australia. Genoa, about 1950

Henri Cartier-Bresson. Wood gatherers in the Basilicata. Italy 1952

Ugo Mulas. Writer Elio Vittorini. Milan 1962

Leonardo Bezzola. At the Pinin Farina coachbuilding workshop. Turin 1958

Bruno Barbey. Frascati. 1962–64

Henri Cartier-Bresson. Dignitaries at the laying of the foundation stone of a factory in the Basilicata. Italy 1952

Herbert List. Film director Vittorio de Sica and actors. Naples 1961

Bruno Barbey. Milan. 1962–64

Bruno Barbey. Naples. 1962–64

Dölf Preisig. Assassination attempt on Pope John Paul II. Rome 1981

Gabriele Basilico. In the old harbour. Trieste 1985

Hans Finsler. Priest blessing fishing boats before departure. Chioggia, Italy 1952

Gianni Berengo Gardin. Roman wedding. 1994

Gotthard Schuh. Lovers in Parco della Rimembranza. Rome 1950

FACE TO FACE

Faces, eyes. We learn by experience that it is the eyes that give the face its particular expression – and its own mystery. But a face can also speak with its eyes closed. And the eyes are not always directed outwards. Sometimes they look inside – and then who knows where, into unknown places.

Herbert List. Painter Giorgio Morandi. Bologna, Italy 1953

Herbert List. Pablo Picasso. Paris 1948

Daniel Schwartz. Friedrich Dürrenmatt. Nuremberg, Switzerland 1990

Lisetta Carmi. Ezra Pound. San Lorenzo, Italy 1966

Christian Vogt. Artist Meret Oppenheim. Basle 1985

René Burri. Ernesto Che Guevara. Havana 1963

THE EUROPEAN EAST

Ways in the European East are difficult, and have been for decades. Stalin's dictatorial communism dominates all of Europe well after his death. In 1953, when Khrushchev comes to power and stays until 1964, Stalin's 'personality cult' starts to crumble, and the slogan 'peaceful co-existence' is coined. 'Détente' is spoken of. But in 1956 the popular uprising in Hungary is brutally repressed; in 1958 the Russians give the Berlin ultimatum; in 1961 the Wall is built; and in 1968 the Soviet army marches into Prague. There is the Gulag Archipelago. And now, after the end of state socialism, the results still cannot be overlooked. Least of all in the Balkans.

Christian Staub. In the Russian Officers' Club in the Hofburg, Vienna. 1946

Anon. Laying the 'Stalinka' railway over the frozen Ob. Western Siberia, about 1950

Thomasz Kizny. Prisoners' shoes at the deserted Gulag 9, west of the Yenisey river. Western Siberia, 1990

Following pages: Werner Bischof. Beggar in Homoród. Romania 1947

Ernst Haas. POWs returning from Russia, Vienna South railway station. 1945–48

Werner Bischof. Romania 1947

Werner Bischof. On the flooded road from Focşani to Galaţi. Romania 1947

Robert Capa. On a collective in the Ukraine. 1947

René Burri. Bus station in front of the Centrum store. Warsaw 1989

Markéta Luskacová. Pilgrims reading the Bible. Slovakia 1967

René Burri. Film director Andrzej Wajda at work. Warsaw 1989

Thomas Kern. Mother with photographs of her four sons, who were evacuated by the Red Cross from a Serbian POW camp in Manjaca to a London hospital. Zenica, central Bosnia, February 1993

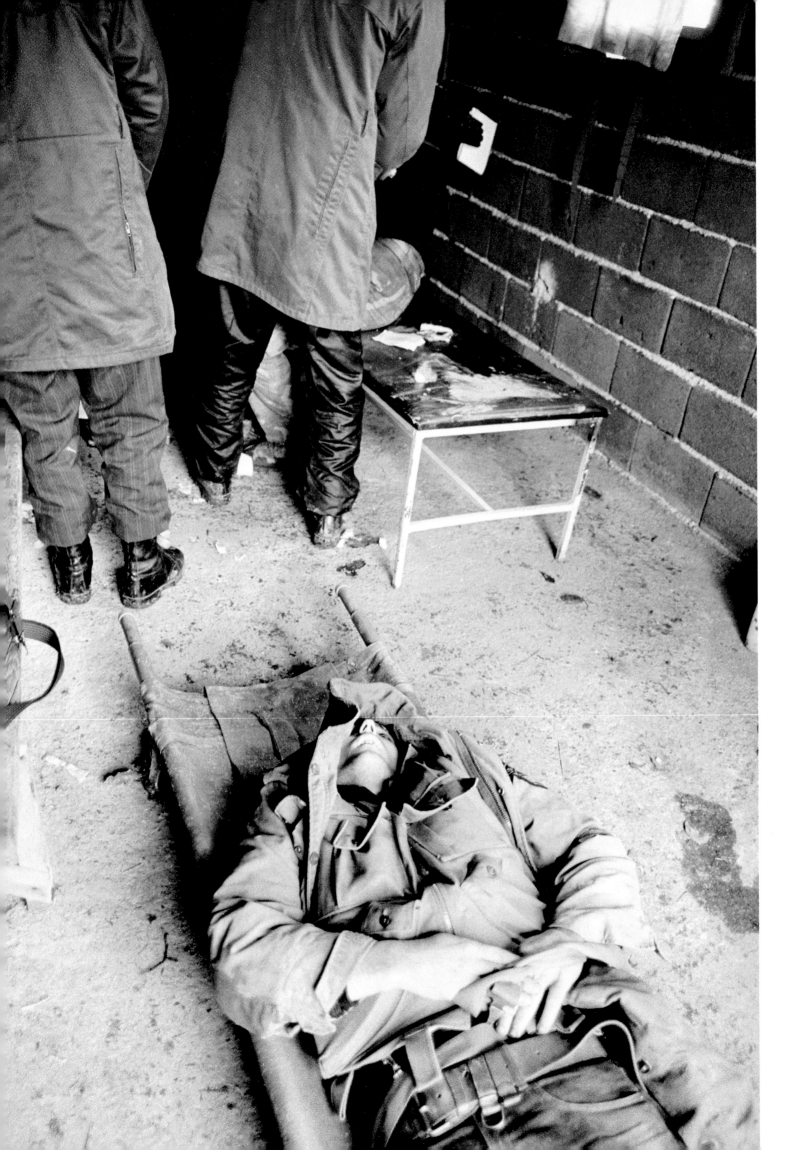

Thomas Kern. Dead Bosnian soldier in a field hospital near Sarajevo. December 1992

Thomas Kern. Bosnian Croat at the front line. Goražde, eastern Bosnia, October 1992

Thomas Kern. Two Bosnian soldiers on the way to the front. Goražde, eastern Bosnia, October 1992

BRIEF ENCOUNTERS

Living together is not just a fact. It is a responsibility. And it is the never-ending job of photography to document living together, next to one another, but also opposed to one another. Endless possibilities of interhuman constellations… mourning and happiness, pain, serenity, love and jealousy – everything with and through the other. To understand oneself in others; the other is… ourselves.

George Hoyningen-Huene. Mae West in the film *It Ain't No Sin*. Hollywood 1934

André Kertész. Constantin Brancusi. Paris 1928

Bruce Davidson. Social worker restrains a young gang member. New York 1959

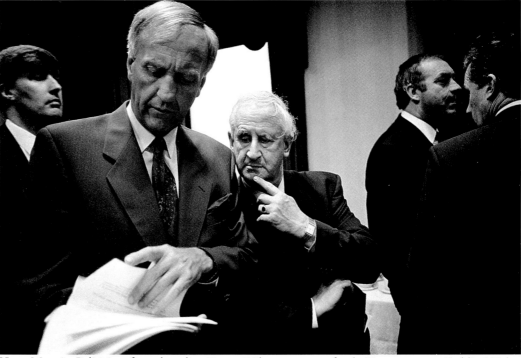

Horst Munzig. Politicians from the ruling Fianna Fáil party prepare for the European vote. Dublin 1994

Brassaï. Quarrel, Bal des Quatre Saisons. Paris about 1932

René Burri. Health Ministry in Rio de Janeiro. Brazil 1960

Nelly Rau-Häring. The actress Astrid Meyerfeldt. Volksbühne, Berlin 1993

Henri Schmid. On the way to church. Witikon, Switzerland 1948

Robert Frank. Michelangelo Antonioni and Monica Vitti filming *Eclisse*. Rome 1961

Dölf Preisig. Friedrich Dürrenmatt at the rehearsals for *Portrait eines Planeten* (Portrait of a Planet). Schauspielhaus, Zurich 1971

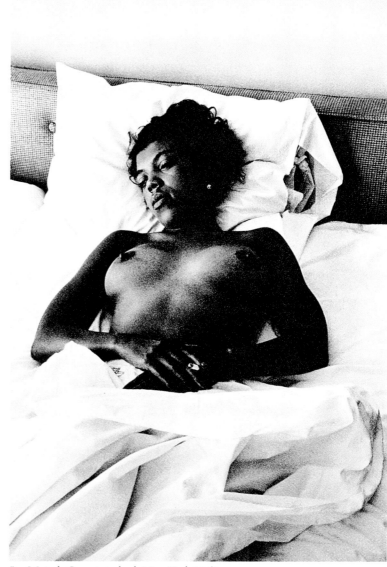

Jay Maisel. Connie in bed. New York 1960

Yvonne Griss. Woman watching television. Zurich 1988

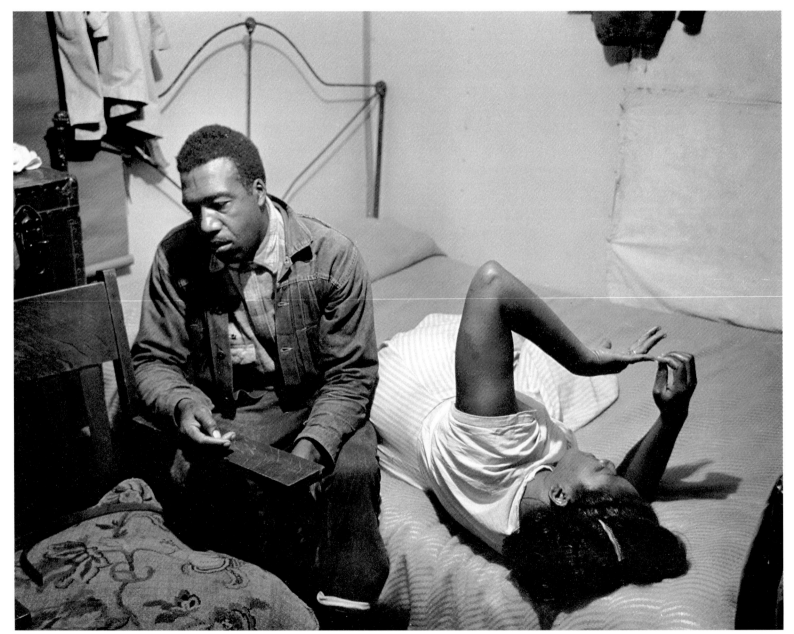

Wayne F. Miller. Cotton-picker and his wife. California 1949

Luigi Realini. Iron sculptor Robert Müller and his family. Paris 1959

IN THE NEAR EAST

An area of unrest, ever since 1918. The opposition of Arabs and Jews, their right to be in the same region, lies at the root of one of the great political conflicts of the twentieth century. The Basle Congress of the Zionist Movement in 1897, held to secure a home in Palestine for the Jewish people, leads eventually to the establishment of the state of Israel in 1948. There is always turbulence, through to the assassination of Premier Rabin by a Jewish radical in 1995: there is not only a multinational, multireligious mix in the eastern Mediterranean, but a collision of old and new ideologies – of different fundamentalisms of the most conflicting kind.

Helmar Lerski. Arab from Palestine. 1931–35

Yvan Dalain. Family of Jewish immigrants arriving at the port of Haifa. Israel 1959

Inge Morath. Distribution of the monthly date ration in the Jericho refugee camp. Jordan 1959

Helmar Lerski. Arab from Palestine. 1931–35

Helmar Lerski. Yemeni Jew from Palestine. 1931–35

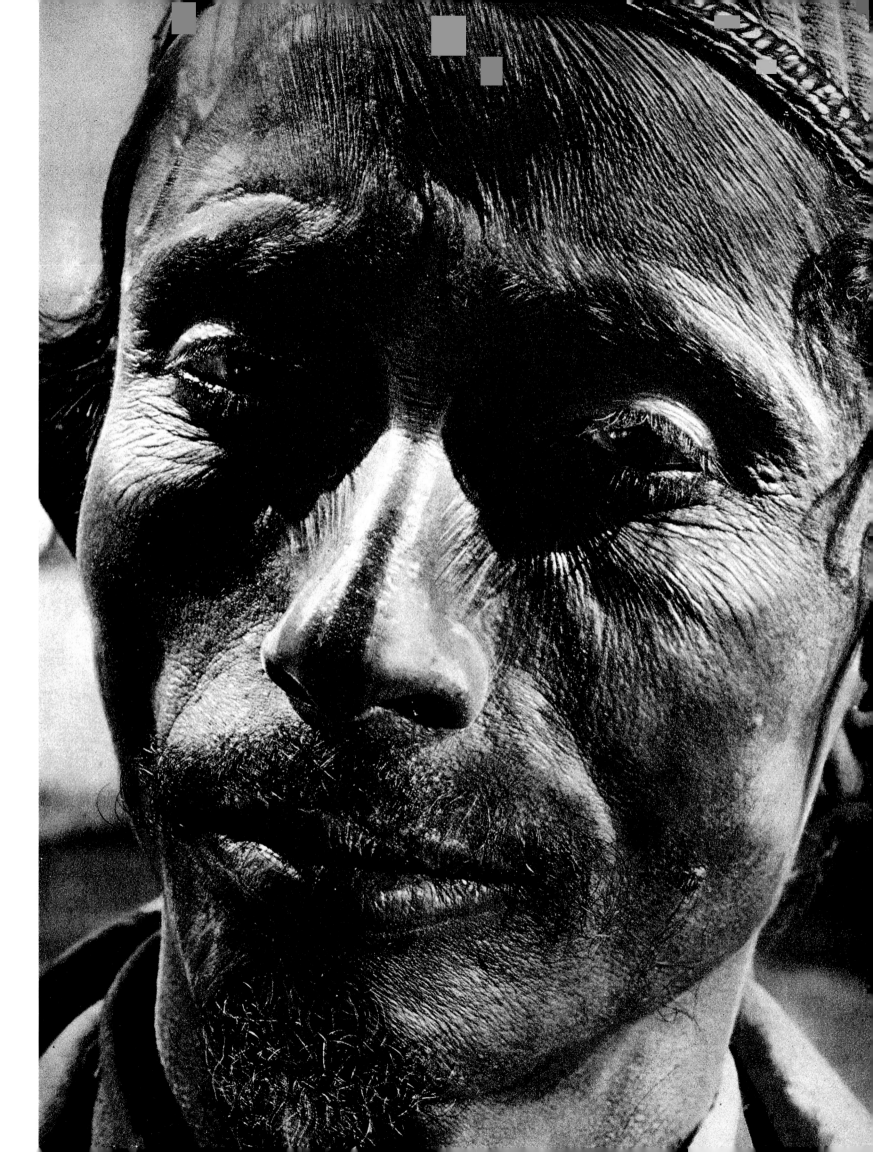

Samer Mohdad. In the Ain Al Heloné camp, Saide, Palestine.

Anon. Immediately before the founding of the State of Israel. In front of the Damascus gate, behind which is the Arab quarter. Jerusalem 1947

Samer Mohdad. In a village on the coast of Al Assad. Syria 1993

Samer Mohdad. In the Faculty of Arabic languages. Al Ashar, Cairo 1994

THE CREATIVE MOMENT

What does art emerge from? From tradition, the summing up of all that has gone before? Or from surpassing, transcending it? To capture the instant of creation: the lonely moment in the atelier, the building site of the work, where individual experience turns over into the register of many, where the work detaches itself from its creator and becomes independent. The gestures, the hand movements, motion and emotion: seeing the outside of a puzzle.

Ugo Mulas. Lucio Fontana making the picture *Attese* (Expectations). Italy 1965

Ed van der Elsken. Karel Appel in Schloss Groeneveld. Baaren, Holland, 1961–62

Hans Namuth. Jackson Pollock with his drip-painting
Autumn Rhythm. East Hampton, Long Island 1950

Ernst Scheidegger. Alberto Giacometti. Paris about 1950

Leonardo Bezzola. Jean Tinguely drawing the first circles for the Stravinsky fountain in Paris.
Bezons, France 1982

Karl Geiser. In the atelier. Zollikon, Switzerland, early 1930s

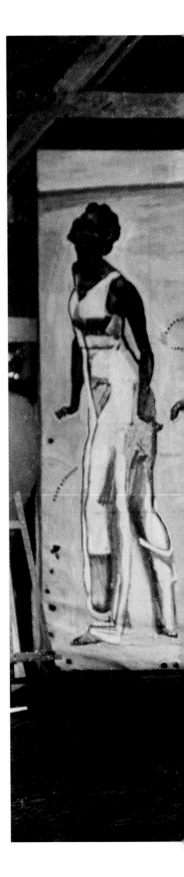

Gertrud Dübi-Müller. Ferdinand Hodler working on his last monumental picture
Blick in die Unendlichkeit (Looking into Infinity). Geneva about 1915

Daniel Schwartz. Otto Müller with his sculpture *Grosser Kopf* (Large Head). Zurich 1990

Vladimir Spacek. Architect Luigi Snozzi in Casa Diener. Ronco, Switzerland 1989

Jean-Pascal Imsand. Artist Stefan Gritsch's pencil.

GO WEST: USA

Nations grow up too. The 'young country of America' has had many experiences in the second half of the twentieth century which have left their mark: Korea, Vietnam, but also internal political catastrophes: the assassination of Kennedy, the civil rights movements and the peace marches of blacks and whites. Growth has come to an end, and even the belief in technological advance is no longer universal. Yet the USA brought the most creative music of the century, jazz, from its beginnings to its universal acceptance, and in the 1960s and 1970s the most important chapters of the history of modern Western art were written here – not to mention film, which was founded as a dream factory and in which the USA are still the leaders. But the American dream at the end of the millennium is played out against a less friendly reality.

Matt Herron. March from Selma to Montgomery during the American Civil Rights campaign. Alabama 1965

Anon. Group of judges at the International Livestock Show. Chicago 1930

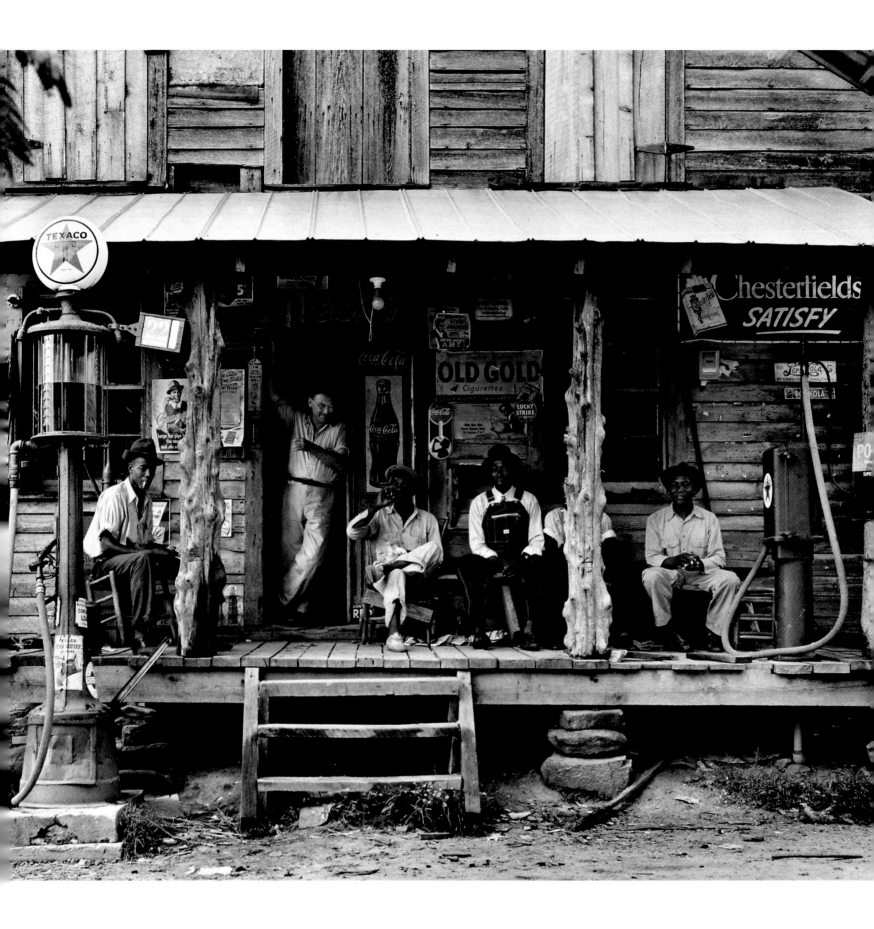

Dorothea Lange. Crossroad store, Alabama 1937

Robert Frank. SS Mauretania. 1953

Robert Frank. St Petersburg, Florida 1955

Robert Frank. Rodeo. Detroit 1955

Bruce Davidson. East 100th Street, New York 1966–68

Ugo Mulas. Marcel Duchamp. New York 1965

Bruce Davidson. Birthday party in Brooklyn. New York 1959

Bruce Davidson. Make up. New York 1959

Dennis Stock. Billie Holiday. 1958

Bruce Roberts. Flaming cross of the Ku-Klux-Klan. New Salisbury, North Carolina 1965

Emil Schulthess. View from Weehawken, New Jersey, across the Hudson River into Manhattan, looking down 42nd Street. New York 1953

Bruce Davidson. East 100th Street, New York 1966–68

Bruce Davidson. East 100th Street, New York 1966–68

Bruce Davidson. East 100th Street, New York 1966–68

Ugo Mulas. John Cage. New York 1954

Giuseppe Pino. Miles Davis. Antibes, France, 1969

Don Hunstein. Glenn Gould trying out a new grand piano. 1957

W. Eugene Smith. Thelonius Monk. About 1960

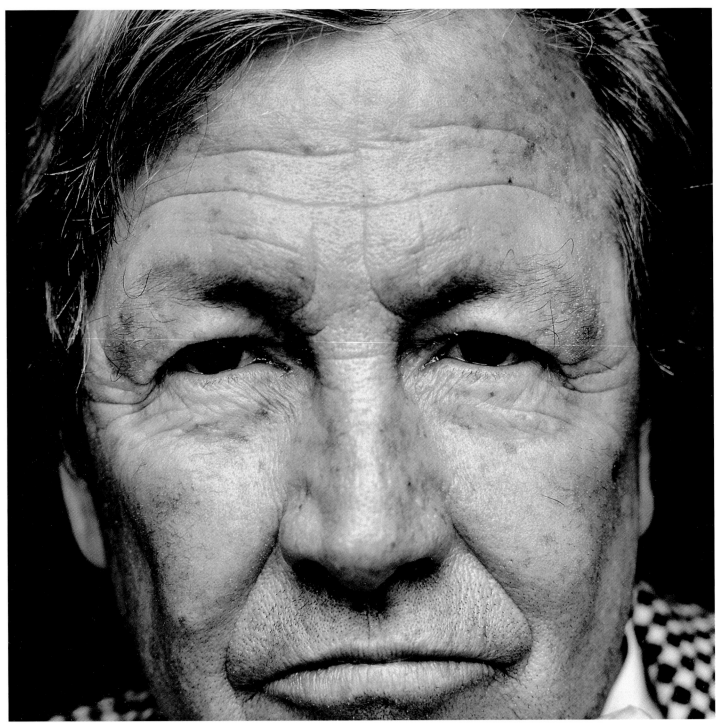

Armin Linke. Robert Rauschenberg. Washington, D.C. 1993

Armin Linke. Jasper Johns. New York 1991

Armin Linke. Artist Robert Morris. New York 1993

Armin Linke. Artist Keith Haring. New York 1988

Bruce Davidson. The ninety-year-old verger Markowitz in the Elridge Street Synagogue. New York 1990

Bruce Davidson. Retired rabbis praying and studying in the Haus der Weisen on East Broadway. New York 1990

Donna Ferrato. Bus on the M5 line, Central Park/Fifth Avenue. New York 1994

Donna Ferrato. Beggar in the financial district. New York 1994

CENTRAL AND SOUTH AMERICA

People spoke of banana republics, and encountered cultures. They saw the gleam of dictatorship, and experienced the misery of the masses. They sowed revolutions, and harvested defeats. A long time ago, people came into a completely unknown world, as conquerors, and so as murderers, and today the broadest mix of peoples, of Indians, blacks and whites, flourishes. South America, between magic and materialism, is a continent whose past does not give away its future.

Werner Bischof. On the way to Cuzco. Peru 1954

Flor Garduño. Writer Juan Rulfo. Mexico, 1983

Gisèle Freund. Evita Perón, wife of the Argentinian president. Buenos Aires 1950

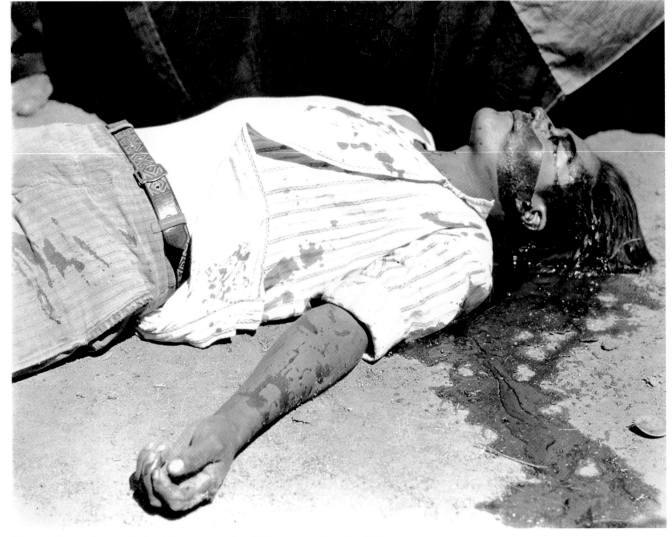

Manuel Alvarez-Bravo. Strike. Murdered worker. Tehuantepec, Mexico 1934

Flor Garduño. Confraternity of the Holy Child. Santiago Atitlán. Guatemala 1989

Flor Garduño. Way to the cemetery. Tixán, Ecuador 1988

René Burri. Bus station in the Regla quarter in the port. Havana 1993

René Burri. Fidel Castro speaking in the Chaplin Theatre at the opening of the Latin American Women's Congress. Havana 1963

René Burri. Havana 1963

René Burri. Shipbuilding in the port. Havana 1963

Flor Garduño. Way to the carnival. Toledo, Bolivia 1990

Flor Garduño. Holy Catholic Church. La Pacifica, Ecuador 1991

UNDER THE SIGN OF THE ANIMAL

Since we have had weapons, animals have been our victims. Since we have eaten, animals have been our food. Since we have built societies, animals have been our companions and helpers. Ultimately, we too are only a certain kind of animal. But we still have to learn that animals that are not human still have some worth. We dominate animals, we can use them, we can destroy them. The writer Elias Canetti said: 'Every animal species that dies makes it less probable that we will live. Only when we consider their forms and voices can we remain human… Animals must become powerful in our thinking again, as in the time before their subjugation.'

Mario Carrieri. On Corso Buenos Aires. Milan, about 1960

Peter Beard. Skinned and sundried carcass with head placed on it. Kenya, about 1965

Fulvio Roiter. Kurds in front of stone relief in Tâq-e Bostân. Iran, early 1960s

Anon. Russian field battery after a German air attack near Smolensk. Russia 1941

Herbert List. Veiled memorial to the king. Athens 1937

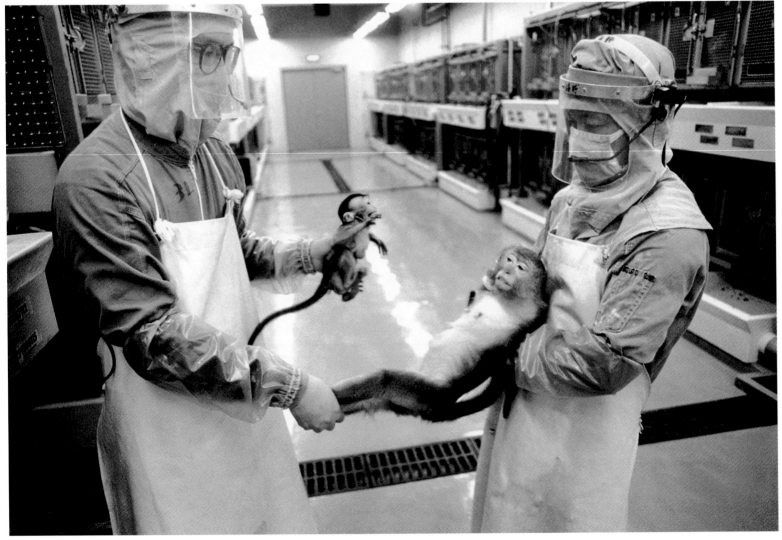

Greg Davis. Experimental laboratory. Tokyo 1993

Hans Hinz. *The War* at the Picasso exhibition in the Palazzo Reale. Milan 1953

Henri Cartier-Bresson. On the way to market. Basilicata, Italy 1952

Peter Beard. Kenya, about 1965

Mario García Joya. Havana 1984

Robert Frank. Porte de Clignancourt. Paris 1952

WORK

Once work meant work in nature: agriculture, keeping livestock, fishing. Work was manual work, manual labour, and that remained the case throughout the time of industrialization, even when now it became mass labour. Admittedly, society acquired a new illness with every new achievement; industrialization meant unemployment. Now that the industrial age is over, work has become invisible. There are no more hands that graft, and there is no more 'sweat on the brow' of our postmodern society. From earlier forms of work, only the illness remains, unemployment, and that is more dangerous than ever.

Jakob Tuggener. Building the dam wall, Oberaar. Switzerland 1953

Jakob Tuggener. Henneberg textile mill. Adliswil, Switzerland 1953

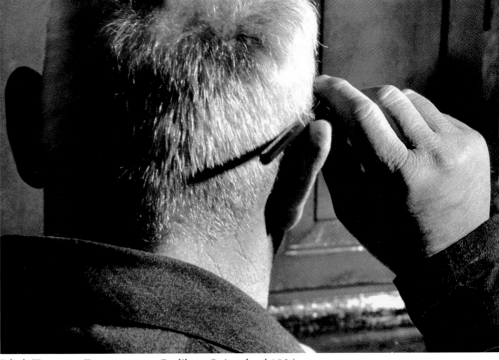

Jakob Tuggener. Factory porter. Oerlikon, Switzerland 1934

Werner Bischof. Smelter at the electric furnace in the
Sulzer Brothers machine factory. Winterthur, Switzerland 1943

Enzo Sellerio. Charcoal burners near Zafferana Etnea. Sicily 1963

Ernst Brunner. Muck-carriers near Mörel in Oberwallis. Switzerland 1941

Bill Brandt. Parlourmaid and under-parlourmaid ready to serve dinner. London, about 1936

Dorothea Lange. White Angel Breadline. San Francisco 1933

Anita Niesz. Steel cable carrier in marble quarry. Carrara, Italy 1955

Henri Cartier-Bresson. On a barge on the Seine. Paris, early 1950s

Rob Gnant. Coal-picker. Borinage, Belgium 1952

Ernst Brunner. Charcoal kiln in Entlebuch. Switzerland 1940

Gisèle Freund. Unemployed miners. Whitehaven, England 1935

Philip Jones Griffiths. The end of the mining village Pont-y-wann. Wales 1961

CULT AND RELIGION

By far the majority of all armed conflicts have been between groups with different religions. Whether religion has been the reason or the excuse is open to question. Conquests are carried out against a background of belief; believers describe the others as non-believers; religions split and define the world. But this much is irrefutable: 'Man cannot live on bread alone.' No person, no society, lives a material life without a metaphysical superstructure, without the mental consciousness of life, fate and death. Religion is rite and cult, in ever-differing, many-sided forms – giving life form in view of the certainty of death.

Herbert List. Ecstatic crowd at voodoo ceremony. Jamaica 1957

George Rodger. Arabian dancer in a trance. Libya 1947

Daniel Schwartz. Shwe Dagon Pagoda. Rangoon, Burma 1991

211

Horst Munzig. Semana Santa. Seville, Spain 1964

Bruno Barbey. Naples 1964

Horst Munzig. Pilgrims on the holy mountain Croagh Patrick. Ireland 1960.

Flor Garduño. Visions at the cemetery. Quiche, Guatemala 1990

Paul Senn. Prayers in the mountains above Evolène in Wallis, Switzerland 1930s

CHILDREN

The history of children is not very old. For a long time children were no more than 'small adults'. Even more recent is the cult of the child, as fostered in Western luxury society. These are not typical patterns in the destiny of the child. Where life is a new struggle every day, children are only labour, or worse: they are victims who share their parents' destiny.

Candid Lang. Untervaz. Switzerland 1950s

Bill Brandt. Circus boy. England, early 1930s

Henri Cartier-Bresson. Seine boatman. France 1953

August Sander. Girl in circus caravan. Cologne 1926

Herbert List. Young Athenian accompanies organ-grinder. Greece 1938

Giorgio Soavi. In Balthus's atelier in the Villa Medici. Rome 1973

René Burri. Schoolboys in front of a shop window with Samurai swords. National Museum, Tokyo 1961

Sabine Weiss. Picasso's son Claude fighting on the way to school. Paris 1954

Daniel Schwartz. Road workers. Rangoon, Burma 1992

Masanori Kobayashi. Refugees of civil war and famine at Boroma in the borderland between Somalia and Ethiopia, 1980

UNDER SURVEILLANCE

Under surveillance, behind walls. Here are monks, children, the handicapped, convicts, the mentally ill, prisoners of war. Most of them are not where they are by choice. Their world is cut off from the outside, another world, an inner space. Pictures bear witness for people we like to forget.

Paul Senn. Patient in the garden of Waldau mental institution. Switzerland 1936

Paul Senn. Noli on the Mediterranean coast. Italy 1948

Ernst Scheidegger. In a reform school. Italy 1948

Carla Cerati. In a mental hospital. Italy, about 1968

Danny Lyon. Prison inmates at work in the woods. Texas 1970

René Burri. Zen monk meditating in front of a stone garden. Japan 1961

Werner Bischof. At Mimi Scheiblauer's deaf and dumb school. Zurich 1944

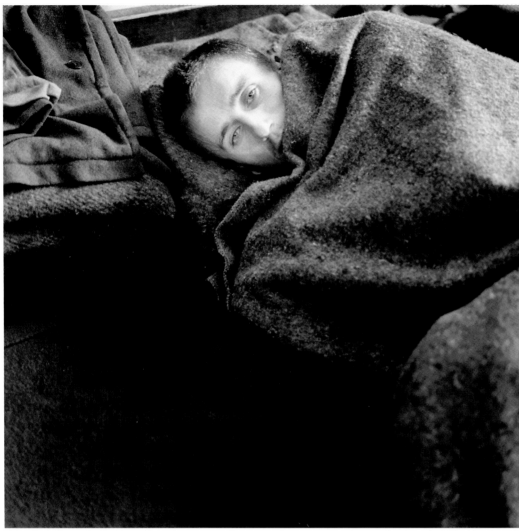

Thomas Kern. In the Serbian POW camp at Manjaca. Bosnia, October 1992

Paul Senn. Prisoners taking their daily midday walk in Thorberg prison. Switzerland 1937

GO EAST: INDIA

The population of the Indian subcontinent will soon exceed one billion. As a bridge between West and East Asia, tradition and religion are as much the key, or mediator, as modernity and industry. India itself lives within the great contrast between the agrarian world of old and towns splitting at the seams; it lives simultaneously with myths and modernity. India, between West and East, is a world of its own.

Werner Bischof. Starving people. Bihar 1951

Werner Bischof. Starving children following vehicles carrying food. Bihar 1951

Henri Cartier-Bresson. Mahatma Gandhi's burning funeral pyre on the Yamuna river. Delhi, 31 January 1948

Deyanita Singh. A Sikh bridegroom waits for his bride. Karnal 1993

Werner Bischof. Workers at the Damodar valley power station, 1951

Rahul Singh. V. S. Naipaul. Calcutta 1988

Manuel Bauer. Tibetan refugee. Delhi 1995

FROM INDOCHINA TO BURMA

The names of the countries and peoples of the old South-East Asia are redolent of both war and misery. Under Japanese protection, the state of Vietnam developed out of Tonkin, Annam and Cochinchina. After the collapse of Japan in 1945, Vietnam became communist under Ho Chi Minh. In 1946 France began its war in Indochina; in 1949, Cambodia, Laos and Vietnam became independent; but France withdrew from the region only in 1954 after its defeat at Dien Bien Phu. In 1954 Vietnam was divided into two sovereign states. From 1957 there were armed clashes between government troops in the South and the communist Viet Cong. The USA sent 'military advisers', and, in 1964, regular troops. The war ended in 1975 with the capitulation of South Vietnam and the withdrawal of the Americans. Vietnam is on the road to normality; Korea remains divided; and Burma is under the control of a military regime.

Werner Bischof. Grave of a fallen Frenchman in Tonkin. Indochina 1952

Daniel Schwartz. Shwe Dagon Pagoda. Rangoon, Burma 1991

Tim Page. After a failed attempt to free North Vietnamese POWs in Bien Hoa camp. South Vietnam 1969

Werner Bischof. Women praying for their husbands at war. Gian Coc, Indochina 1952

Marc Riboud. Schoolchildren leaving village school. North Vietnam 1968–69

Werner Bischof. Sick Chinese POWs in Koje-do camp. Korea 1952

Hiroji Kubota. Americans on Okinawa with dogs for deployment in the Vietnam war. Japan 1969

JAPAN

When the photographer Werner Bischof went to Tokyo for the first time in 1951, six years had passed since the dropping of the atomic bombs on Hiroshima and Nagasaki. Bischof saw the victims; he saw what had been preserved of Japan's classical culture; he saw monks in the snow. Ten years later René Burri saw a more urban culture – and the beginning of that economic explosion which today is synonymous with Japan.

Shomei Tomatsu. From the series 'Signs of rapid economic growth'. 1971

Hiroshi Hamaya. Sand carriers resting. Honshu, 1954–57

William Klein. Bubble ceremony. Tokyo 1961

René Burri. Silk drying. 1961

Werner Bischof. War casualty. Tokyo 1951

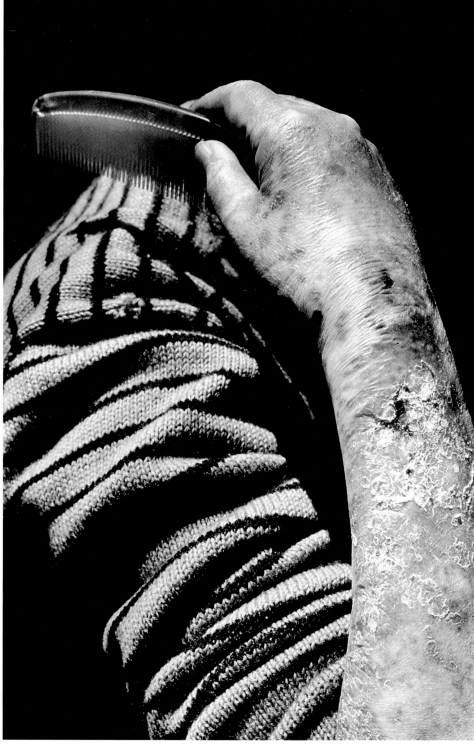

Shomei Tomatsu. From the series '11:02 Nagasaki'. 1962

Werner Bischof. Striptease artist in her dressing room. Tokyo 1951

René Burri. Actress being made up for a male role in the geisha theatre. Kyoto 1961

Werner Bischof. Shinto priests in the inner courtyard
of the Meiji temple. Tokyo 1952

CHINA AND TIBET

Of all the peoples in the world, China has remained the Unknown for the longest time. In the past, protected by walls which kept foreigners out just as it kept the Emperor's kingdom together, China was, until only a few years ago, isolated in an ideological radicalism without comparison. Of every country in the world China has gone its own way for the longest; always a way of attempted cultural identity, but also of hegemony and suppression (as can be seen today in Tibet). Only right at the end of the twentieth century has China opened up – and appears threatening to the West: as an economic superpower.

Henri Cartier-Bresson. Procession of Communist Party sympathizers through the streets of Shanghai. 1 August 1949

Robert Capa. Hankou after destruction by Japanese napalm bombs. China 1938

René Burri. May Day parade on the bridge in front of the Gate of Heaven. Beijing 1964

Joan Lebold Cohen. Nude class at the Guangzhou academy. China 1979–80

Marc Riboud. Bridge-building on the Yangtze. China 1957

Manuel Bauer. Tibetan pilgrims and soldiers of the Chinese People's Liberation Army. Lhasa, Tibet 1955

Manuel Bauer. Tibetan ragpickers in the outskirts of Lhasa. Tibet 1955

Manuel Bauer. Tibetan refugees after crossing the Himalayas on the way to freedom. Nepal 1955

TERRITORIES

Surface. Inanimate Nature. Scene. Stage. Mother Earth. The patient planet.

Albert Steiner. 'Of valleys and people': view from Fuorcla Crast'Agüzza to Engadin. Switzerland 1920s

Auguste-Rosalie Bisson. Climbing from Chamonix up Mont Blanc. France, July 1861

Edouard Widmer. Burial mound of Antiochus I of Commagene, Nimrud Dâg. Turkey 1960

Constantin Brancusi. Brancusi's *La Colonne sans fin* (The Endless Column) in Targu Jiu. Romania 1937

Daniel Schwartz. The Great Wall of China at Jiuquam. 1987

The Real Moment: Dieter Bachmann
Permanence in change: du *magazine and its photographers through half a century*

It was spring, the war was over. In May 1946 *du* magazine published a portrait of a little Dutch boy on its cover. It was not the usual pleasant picture of a child. In fact, it was something of a test of courage; 'we were not sure about this picture, nor did we all agree,' admitted the editor-in-chief Arnold Kübler two months later. The picture did arouse sympathy in the magazine's readers: but it also aroused disapproval, anger, horror. Dramatically cropped, it showed the face of a boy perhaps ten years old. His right eye was made of glass, the result of a fire; his skin was covered in countless tiny scars, 'turned blue by the cold of the morning at 12 degrees below freezing'.

Late in the autumn of 1945, not many months after a war which had ravaged Europe from one end of the continent to the other, two Swiss photographers set off by car on a journey through France, Belgium and Holland: Werner Bischof, twenty-nine years old, and Emil Schulthess, about the same age. Bischof's assignment was to record Europe's war damage. He had proposed it himself, but the magazine supported him. The contract stated that he would have a car and a colour camera at his disposal. 'All other travelling expenses are the responsibility of Herr Bischof.' Bischof's brief was made clear in Clause 6: 'People and their behaviour in the resulting chaos are to be included.'

Bischof and Schulthess saw the injured boy when they reached Roermond in Holland, though they did not manage to photograph this example of 'behaviour in the resulting chaos' straight away. But he had made an impression on them. Several weeks later, on their return journey, they made a detour to look for him again. Bischof photographed him in colour against the wall of a house. In the May 1946 issue, devoted to 'Werner Bischof's European photographs', Kübler wrote: 'he was injured by one of those small, wooden-cased mines the size of a pencil, which the retreating Germans left in their thousands. These things were concealed in apartments, in boxes, baskets, corridors, attached to door latches, just to make things generally dangerous, and the boy was hit by the explosion when he came home after an air raid and innocently opened the door of the apartment.'

Did the magazine want to cause a sensation with this issue? Yes. A scandal? No. Its concern was for something else, something at the time typical for the magazine. The word for it was solidarity. The premise was shock: 'One cannot read it without being deeply shaken,' wrote Kübler in the same issue, ' and without realizing how much in our protected surroundings we are prone to indifference.' This Dutch boy should have jolted our hearts: 'Hundreds of thousands of children in Europe have lost fathers, mothers, brothers and sisters. Some have lost even their names and identities … These children are a part of the Europe of the future; when they grow up they will have to live with memories in their hearts of a childhood spent so close to our country, in a world that is no older than they are … The various Swiss aid organizations have already given a great deal of help; but there is no such thing as enough.'

du devoted three whole issues to the destruction in Europe (as well as separate contributions in many other issues). One of these, the May 1946 issue, has several more black and white photographs by Bischof which later became world famous: for example, the picture of the boy in Maastricht playing with a piece of string, a wickerwork basket at his feet, or the hospital train with returning Italians in Merano. Many other photographs by Bischof from this time in other issues and from other countries – Italy, Greece, Romania, Hungary, Czechoslovakia, Poland, Finland, Sweden and Denmark, all taken between 1945 and 1949 – have become icons.

It is surely remarkable that a magazine should in those days have been willing to let a photographer work on the same assignment for several months: and that so much of his material should have been published. But the magazine, already committed to focusing on cultural and natural scientific themes, was ready to give considerable space and weight to social and political reporting. And in this case it had spotted a photographer who was to grow to be one of the most important of all Swiss photographers. Photography, after all, had been a key feature of *du* ever since it was founded in 1941.

Bischof became one of the first freelance photographers to be regularly promoted by the magazine, and before long, and even after he had attained international recognition, *du* became a sort of home port for him. Today he remains the man responsible for the magazine's commitment to photography: he set a standard for all those who have followed. *du* has published Ernst Haas's colour experiments, Lucien Clergue's studies, and many innovations following the work of Man Ray, but has come back again and again to documentary photography, photography dedicated to the 'real moment', to human fate on this patient planet. It shows joy and misery, the great and the nameless; it gives a voice to those who have no voice.

Two months after the appearance of the disturbing cover with the Dutch boy, Arnold Kübler wrote the following thoughtful reply to those who had seen in its publication only an aberration of taste: 'To the accusation of tastelessness we alone are answerable. The cries of the miserable have never been to the taste of those who are safe and happy. Taste? What is that? What is it next to truth, love, sacrifice? Was taste the reason why we printed this picture?'

Arnold Kübler was an unusual figure. Born in 1890 in a rural district outside Winterthur near Zurich, he studied geology, wanted to become a sculptor and then an actor; he became a writer, and then a journalist by force of circumstance: he had a family to support. 'When I came back home from Berlin, not exactly covered with glory, and settled down in Zurich, I found a crafty solution: I had myself made head of a paper, albeit only a picture paper, the sort where good writing was outshone by mediocre photography.'

Kübler could not allow this situation to continue. The *Zürcher Illustrierte* became the first Swiss magazine to learn to handle the still new medium of photoreportage. Kübler took on a new generation of photographers: Hans Staub, Paul Senn, Ernst Mettler, Emil Schulthess and, of course, Werner Bischof. 'The *ZI* was the paper for young Swiss photography.' In 1933 the *ZI* had the honour of being the first Swiss newspaper to be banned in Germany; but in 1941 the publishers Conzett & Huber closed it down ('the Great War broke out. Advertising dried up.'). In its place they founded a monthly magazine, largely in order to utilize their own high-quality colour presses. Kübler was to be its first editor-in-chief.

Opinion was divided over the title for the new magazine. 'There was,' he wrote, 'a shower of suggestions from all sides: *Conzett & Huber's Monthly*, *Thirty Days*, *Tictac*, *Red Raven*, *Impulse*, *Profile*, *Swiss Cross-section*, *Elan*. *Elan*, favoured by female colleagues, had the best chances of winning. It had the majority of the management votes. Clear opposition came from just one person, who hadn't been asked, the magazine's future chief – me. I explained I was incapable of running or wanting to run a magazine with that name. So I suggested *du*. Challenging title, a word which speaks of openness, of affection for the world, for people, material things, nature.'

With the help of handwritten drafts, which Emil Schulthess sketched in several different ways throughout the night for a decision by the management committee, the two men succeeded in getting the title through. The first issue appeared in March 1941. The founding of such a sophisticated and expensive magazine seems notably courageous at a time when Switzerland resembled an island, completely surrounded by fascist or fascist-occupied countries. In his first editorial Kübler justifies the unusual title in the context of the current political situation. 'The title is not based in the slightest on forced intimacy. *du* is not simply a impertinent notion, it is an agenda. Any lack of respect is far from our thoughts. Everyone realizes: we live in a time of great upheaval and displacement. The world is caught in an ice-drift… Every day calls out to us: You are not alone! You are not just here for your own sake. You have responsibilities and duties beyond those of your own personal inclinations and disinclinations. That is what our title *du* is all about.'

Kübler continued his collaboration with photographers and photography from the first issue. Much of what *du* published had necessarily to do with defending the official doctrine of neutrality. If, for instance, there was an issue on the theme of 'The Cow', with much wonderful photography of the sublime Alpine world, there were also articles which took account of what went on in the outside world: 'Where Does the Name "Europe" Come From?' (April 1941), 'Some Masterpieces of French Painting' (December 1942), 'The Building of the Universe' (December 1943). In its early years *du* was a magazine of mixed interests, focusing on society, culture and knowledge.

Great photographic series still stand out today. But more and more, it is individual pictures that draw attention, are carefully gathered and selected. New names emerge, for instance Jakob Tuggener and Ernst Brunner. Tuggener's vivid black and white photographs have shaped the character of the magazine, which, in the years up to the end of the war and partly after it, bore a remarkably close attachment to a country and to a people. His pictures of a hotel chambermaid making up a guest's bed, of a chic ball in the luxury Baur au Lac hotel in Zurich, of the work on the Oberaar dam, of a Pablo Casals concert and a grandiose photograph of children cutting peat – all these belong together, since, for all their diversity, they depict a closed world, the 'island' of Switzerland, a continuity. The related pictures by Ernst Brunner similarly record the agrarian world of the countryside, the world of farmers and manual labourers – Brunner belonged to a long forgotten generation of photographers: until *du*, in fact, rediscovered him ('Craftsmen', July 1990).

Werner Bischof was one of the 'permanent freelance photographers' on the magazine's staff from February 1942. With Emil Schulthess he was responsible for the photography of the April 1944 issue, 'The invalid'. This issue of the magazine was a decisive step in his turning towards socially committed reportage that became his main work from then on. In February 1945 a special issue appeared containing his photographs on 'Refugees', then between December 1945 and June 1949 the three issues on Europe after the war. With that Bischof's Swiss and European work for *du* was basically concluded.

In May 1949 Bischof married Rosellina Mandel (later the wife of René Burri) and joined the Magnum photo agency; together they set up a Magnum office in Zurich. With them and with Magnum Paris and New York, *du* established a friendly alliance over the next few decades, especially during the editorship of Manuel Gasser and Hugo Loetscher. The Magnum founding members Robert Capa and Henri Cartier-Bresson have worked repeatedly and intensively with and on behalf of *du*; so subsequently have Inge Morath, Bruce Davidson, Sebastião Salgado and others – and especially René Burri, whose first contribution was an issue on Argentinian gauchos in March 1959.

In 1951 Bischof embarked on a long journey through Asia, which took him to India and Japan, and from there to Korea, Hong Kong and Indochina. He reported for *Life* and *Match*. In June 1953 his epoch-making issue of *du* appeared: 'People in the Far East'. It was a brilliant selection of pictures, texts and drawings by Bischof himself, one of those outstanding issues that can only be produced by long experience, a photographer at the height of his creative powers and much good fortune. In September 1953 Bischof travelled by sea to the United States. He went to Panama, Lima, Santiago de Chile, and then up into the Andes, where at about midday on 16 May 1954 he was tragically killed in a road accident.

No one could replace Werner Bischof, but other remarkable photographers produced notable work. In December 1950 Emil Schulthess, who was not only the magazine's designer but also a photographer, published his meticulously prepared record of the course of the midnight sun in twenty-four pictures. The publication aroused worldwide interest; it was republished by *Life*, and in 1952 Schulthess was give the US Camera Award. Encouraged by his success, Schulthess completed two big projects of a type never again to be undertaken by *du*. Travelling across the USA like a discoverer and pioneer in 1954, he reported in five issues: 'By Road Through the United States', November 1954; 'From American Zoos', January 1955; 'An American Cross-section', March 1955; 'American National Parks', April 1955; 'The City of New York', July 1955. It is very likely that Robert Frank knew about Schulthess's enterprise. And in his submission for the Guggenheim fellowship which was to enable him to photograph *The Americans*, Frank included a recommendation by Arnold Kübler. However, it was Robert Delpire in Paris, a close friend of *du*'s then publisher Richard Herzer, who first published *The Americans*. Later, Schulthess crossed the African continent in a similar way from north to south in the winter of 1956–57: four issues in seven months ('The Desert', July 1957, 'French Equatorial Africa and the Congo', May 1957; 'The African Kingdom', September 1957; 'East and South Africa', November 1957).

When Arnold Kübler stepped down in 1957, after sixteen years, the character and standard of photography at *du* were absolutely established. It was a unique blend of vision and selectivity, of social commitment and courageous design; it printed individual pictures large on the page (there lay its difference from the narrative picture sections of other big illustrated magazines); it had a special love of surprise, of the out-of-the-way event, and the droll; and it was unflagging in its attention to detail. All of this was so deeply ingrained that even Kübler's successors with quite different temperaments and interests have never quite been able to distance themselves from this model. The circumstances of Kübler's leaving *du* have never been fully explained. It seems that the management took his vague expression of 'wanting change' as a pretext for getting rid of their inconvenient editor-in-chief. He went with a spring in his step. He never undertook anything else on behalf of *du*, and *du* did not concern itself any more with Kübler – until a special issue appeared in March 1991 to mark his magazine's fiftieth anniversary: 'Homage to Arnold Kübler'.

Kübler was a poet, a political satirist and an amateur artist. In 1965 at the age of seventy-five he undertook a 500-kilometre journey on foot from Paris to Basle, making notes and sketches along the way. His restless spirit, liberated in old age, basked in the air of foreignness and adventure. 'A journey is like life,' he noted in France. 'At the edge of the road grasses grow high, unmown; the wind plays with them and they throw their dancing shadows in ever-changing patterns far across the road which lies before my feet. A lightness has come over me such as I have ever known before, and just breathing is a pleasure.'

Emil Schulthess's American and African issues of *du* of 1954–57 were outstanding examples of something uniquely important for the magazine: the themed issue – a number devoted to a single topic, appearing not as a special issue but as a normal number of *du*. In hindsight, one can say that Kübler had invented it, more by chance than by intention. In its first months, according to Kübler, the magazine had to live so much from hand to mouth that it worked 'at random, without any editorial preparation worth mentioning… After some months an extraordinary event took the worried journalists by surprise: a series of small-format colour photographs were sent in by a connoisseur showing the "Dance of Death" paintings by Jakob von Wyl, done in 1615 for the Lucerne Jesuit college, hanging in the corridors of the Lucerne government building… The editors quickly decided to devote the whole colour section of one issue to these paintings. And the rest of the issue? What could hold its own next to this heavyweight theme? Nothing! Nothing prepared previously, nothing planned for future issues! So it became an issue with a single theme: death.'

The 'Dance of Death' issue appeared in November 1941, the first year of publication. Surprisingly, said Kübler, this opened a new avenue: 'A single subject, clearly outlined, treated just once, but requiring depth, knowledge, seriousness.' 'Everything can become

a *du* thing if only it can be thoroughly grasped in some visual form.' The first themed issues were 'Water', 'The Cow', 'Young Woman', 'Cat and Dog', 'Bees and Honey Bees', 'Swiss Private Collections', (the most important issues of the early 1950s), 'The Air', 'The Maid', but also 'Children in the War'.

None of these issues was conceived as a photonumber – but in each one the photographic contribution was essential for the development and representation of the theme. It was precisely here that *du* developed a specific pictorial language. Since the whole magazine was in those days one big piece of reportage, the editors were searching less for classic photoreportage (narrative picture composition) than for the telling individual picture, whose function could be as a self-contained contribution on a narrative level. Kübler and his crew developed a sort of counterpoint technique, setting picture against text, photograph against theme, so that a photograph played around a theme and reflected it from other perspectives. One example among many: in the 'Water' issue (July 1942) one stumbles with surprise across a black and white agency photograph of – sand. The caption reads: 'Italian tank in the sea of sand of the Libyan desert.' The context of the desert – sea of sand – sea – water has to be supplied mentally by the observer – and when one comes back to the picture, it takes on quite another aspect.

'Themed issues' based on photography, not 'photo-issues'. Themed issues make up about half of all the numbers published in Kübler's era. Photography always plays its part; sometimes it has the lion's share, as in Werner Bischof's issues on postwar Europe. But it was only in June 1952, after eleven years, that *du* made photography itself the subject of an issue, 'Early Swiss photography 1859–1900'. And not until 1952 did an issue appear that was devoted to contemporary photography, precisely the photography in fact which Kübler had been nurturing in his magazine for years: November 1955, 'The Family of Man. People like us'. It came about in the following way. In November 1954 Kübler had visited the seventy-five-year-old Edward Steichen in New York. He was busy putting together what was to be a world-famous exhibition. Out of 10,000 pictures, 503 had been selected; against the walls stood the card-mounted photographs with, Kübler reported, 'pictures put next to each other in endless telling and effective combinations'. Kübler suggested to Steichen, who had visited the *du* offices the year before, looking for good young photographers, that he select material for a *du* issue. Even Kübler must have been somewhat amazed at Steichen's answer: 'A *du* issue? It would be the achievement of a lifetime.' The November 1955 issue contained 35 photographs from Steichen's exhibition.

Yet Kübler was not interested in promoting photographers as objects of personality cults. Shortly before the end of his time at *du*, he devoted an issue (January 1957) to industrial photographs by Jakob Tuggener. Tuggener's pictures might easily have filled the whole issue, but opposite them Kübler placed insect drawings by Walter Linsenmaier – as if he wanted to emphasize that even he, the great discoverer, the tireless pioneer and judge of his photographers, could relegate photography to a modest and subservient role.

It was only under the next editor, Manuel Gasser (1957–73), that purely photographic monograph issues appeared. In the emerging crisis besetting large illustrated magazines *du* became a unique and a gradually more insular medium for committed contemporary photography. Under Gasser's successors this trend continued.

Henri Cartier-Bresson had already published some of his China pictures with Kübler (January 1951). But it was Gasser who devoted a whole issue to his Seine pictures (June 1958); Gasser also published his incomparable portraits of the French intelligentsia (April 1961), his report on the Basilicata region of Italy (July 1974) and (on commission) a work on Switzerland (August 1967). The magazine's continuing work with Cartier-Bresson (e.g. his 1992 photograph of Balthus) is just one example of how such a relationship can endure for decades and through changing circumstances. Others are Herbert List, Horst Munzig, Bruce Davidson, René Burri and, among the youngest, Daniel Schwartz.

It was Manuel Gasser who discovered the young René Burri for *du*. His work on Argentinian gauchos (March 1959) was the beginning of a collaboration that has endured for nearly forty years. Indeed, Burri has published more photographs in the magazine than anyone else. In August 1961 his pictures of Japan appeared; later came Le Corbusier in Paris, Bahia, Jerusalem, Chicago, China, and Warsaw (February 1990) and his great retrospective of thirty years of Cuba (December 1993). Burri, endlessly curious, restless, inexhaustibly enthusiastic for the photographic medium, is like a boxer sparring with his theme. If anyone can embody 'the *du* photographer', that person is René Burri.

For every photographer the long effort of a themed issue is a both an opportunity and a challenge. After working out the theme with the editors, many other issues arise: its scope and limits, type of interpretation, time frame and so on. After Cartier-Bresson's issue on the Seine (and partly in direct continuity with his work) a whole series of issues developed which were only possible within the framework of this particular magazine, for instance: 'New York – 100th Street' by Bruce Davidson (March 1969); 'The Photographer Herbert List' (July 1973); Horst Munzig's Italian issue; and René Burri's Japan.

The editors responsible for the shape of the magazine since 1988, who have decided firmly in favour of the principle of the themed issue over the *ad hoc*-journalism of many magazines, have also taken up its photographic tradition with vigour. In the last few years a whole series of photographic themed issues have appeared: Daniel Schwartz's 'The Great Wall of China – an Idea' (June 1989) and 'Burma 1992. A Report' (November 1992), Horst Munzig's 'The Po. A Cultural Landscape' (November 1990) and 'Dublin. The Dubliners. Reading Joyce in Dublin' (March 1995), Sebastião Salgado's 'World of Perfume' (October 1991), Flor Garduño's 'South American Indians' (January 1992), René Burri's 'Los Cubanos' (December 1993), Armin Linke's 'Face to Face. 57 Faces of Art' (January 1994), and Manuel Bauer's 'Tibet. The Long Road' (July 1995). In addition we should mention a whole series of very great photographs from the former Yugoslavia by the young Zurich photographer Thomas Kern (May 1993).

Both the aesthetic appeal and the commercial success of such photographic 'major undertakings' are evident. But does the magazine have a social responsibility as well? *du* has a very large readership; its current circulation is 30,000, not counting the many hands through which it passes afterwards. Walter Benjamin, the German cultural philosopher whose *Work of Art in the Age of Mechanical Reproduction* is often quoted, said of the photographer Atget: 'With Atget, photographs become standard evidence for historical occurrences, and acquire a hidden political significance.' *du* has no definite socio-political stance. The only criterion in the selection of photographers and their work is quality. But the 'hidden political significance' of work such as Bruce Davidson's '100th Street', Thomas Kern's 'Balkans' or Daniel Schwartz's 'Burma' is too obvious to need comment.

Over the course of the years and decades, without conscious intention, a sort of family of photographers has come together. They do not have family reunions, and they do not share a common

code. As Cartier-Bresson said in 1990: 'You know the relations between photographers are a little like those between ships: they meet each other at sea and exchange a long "toooot" in order to greet one another, but they don't tie up alongside.' This book and the exhibition *Der Geduldige Planet* (The Patient Planet) constitute the first ever reunion of *du* photographers: what unites them is simply the character of the magazine, and the continuous progress of photographic research. *du* – in contrast to magazines such as *Life* – has been published without interruption since it was founded in 1941. Although *du* cannot be said to have a philosophy of photography, it has in the course of time published more and more issues devoted to the particular problems encountered by photographers –the issue, for instance, on Hans Finsler, the Zurich teacher, theoretician and pioneer – 'Hans Finsler: the picture of photography' (March 1964). Again and again there have been individual articles which examined photography theoretically; most recently Marco Meier in 'The visibility of the world. From Baudelaire and Benjamin to Barthes' (July–August 1992, 'Old photographs from the Herzog collection'). But *du* has never held a single ideological position. It has been its pragmatic approach, as well as the various editors' love of photography, that has fostered the close relationship between photography and the magazine. Should we say, it has been an affair of the heart, not the head?

Nevertheless, it is true that certain principles have crystallized themselves which have never openly been discussed, never conclusively formulated and never written down; *du* has a history of dealing with photography, but not a doctrine.

For all *du* pictures (and this includes those assembled here), these words from Robert Frank's 1962 issue ring true: 'Photography must contain one thing: the humanity of the moment.' That is a truly general formula but an applicable one. 'There is nothing in the world that does not have a decisive moment', as Cartier-Bresson said, quoting Cardinal Retz. And he went on, 'the photographer has to observe reality, to capture it, but not to fiddle about with it, neither with the photograph itself nor later in the lab.' That may seem a conservative rule, but it has grown out of photo-reportage assignments. For *du*, it showed, consciously or not, the way that the magazine still follows today – and this selection is its express confirmation.

du has always felt that its first obligation is to people – to people first and art second, and not the other way round. The artist will emerge through the process. The foremost rule for every magazine of this kind must be that of mediation, of communication, and when it does this on a cultural level, then it also automatically does so on a political level. That is, it has and assumes responsibility, whether it speaks the 'language' of photography or some other language. We agree once more with Cartier-Bresson: 'The contraction of thought, as represented by the language of photography, is a great power; but since we always judge according to what we see, a serious question of responsibility arises. Between the public and us there is the medium – the newspaper, the illustrated magazine. The photographer merely delivers the raw material.'

du is aware of that responsibility. For us, photographs are not just the raw material. They are a narrative of humanity, which together we must transmit, distribute and interpret. For an unbroken fifty-four years that has been our mission and our achievement.

Dieter Bachmann

Biographies of the Photographers

Aigner, Lucien
(b. 1901 Hungary) America
After studying in Prague and Berlin Aigner became a photojournalist in the early 1920s. He worked in Hungary, and then in Paris from 1931 until he emigrated to the United States in 1939. He established his reputation in the United States with photo-essays for the *New York Times*, *Look* and many other publications. After retiring from photography for several decades, he returned in the early 1970s as a professional photographer and film-maker. He has been acknowledged as a pioneer of the 35 mm candid camera.
Lucien Aigner (New York: ICP Library of Photographers, 1979)
Aigner's Paris (Stockholm: Museum of Modern Art, 1982)
Aigner's Paris 50 Years Later (Dalton, 1987)

Alvarez-Bravo, Manuel
(b. 1902) Mexico
Born in Mexico to a family of photographers and painters, Alvarez-Bravo began to photograph in 1924. After working as a camera assistant on Sergei Eisenstein's film *Que Viva Mexico!* in 1931, he began to earn his living as a photographer. This led to his first exhibition (1932), his first film (1934) and his first book (1935). He met Paul Strand, Henri Cartier-Bresson and André Breton and exhibited with Surrealist artists. In 1947 he began to teach film-making and photography and through his numerous books and exhibitions of his work, he has become one of the most influential photographers in Latin America.
Jane Livingston. *Manuel Alvarez Bravo* (Washington: Corcoran Gallery, 1978)
Manuel Alvarez-Bravo (Mexico City: Academia de Artes, 1980)

Barbey, Bruno
(b. 1941 Morocco) France
Barbey he worked as photographer for the *Atlas des Voyages* of Editions Rencontre in Lausanne. A member of Magnum from 1968, Barbey·has worked as a photojournalist mainly in areas of political unrest and in the Third World. After spending two years in Poland, in 1982 he organized the *Terre de Guerre* exhibition with René Burri at the Magnum gallery in Paris. He continues to publish photo-essays, mainly from Africa and the Far East, for *Life*, *National Geographic*, *Geo*.
Polen (Hamburg: Hoffmann und Campe, 1982)
Le Gabon (Paris: Editions du Chêne, 1984)

Basilico, Gabriele
(b. 1944) Italy
After studying architecture in Milan, Basilico became a freelance photographer for periodicals such as *Domus* and *Abitare* and for commercial companies. At the same time he has spent years photographing industrial landscapes. In 1991 he collaborated with René Burri and Robert Frank, among others, documenting the centre of Beirut at a crucial period of its history. In 1994–95 Basilico also took part in the DATAR Mission Photographique in France.
Milano. Ritratti di fabbriche (1983)
Porti di mare (1990)
Beyrouth (Paris: Editions du Cyprès, 1992)

Bauer, Manuel
(b. 1966) Switzerland
Bauer trained in the studio of Thomas Cugini and at the Schule für Gestaltung in Zurich (1983–87). After a brief period as an assistant to Cugini, he became a freelance photojournalist. He first undertook social documentary reportage from Egypt, England and Norway, then mainly from India, the United States and the theatres of war in former Yugoslavia. In 1989 he made a documentary film about blind people in sport. In 1990 he co-founded the agency Lookat Photos in Zurich. Bauer has also worked on long-term projects and mounted exhibitions on issues such as Sri Lankan and Tibetan refugees and culture in exile.

Beard, Peter H.
(b. 1938) America
Beard visited Africa for the first time in 1955. After he had completed his training as a draughtsman and woodcutter at Yale University in New Haven (USA), he settled in Kenya in 1961. He has developed an intense interest in the life of people and animals on the African continent.
The End of the Game (London: Thames and Hudson, 1988)

Berengo Gardin, Gianni
(b. 1930) Italy
Berengo-Gardin's career in photography began in 1954. He is a member of the photographers' groups La Gondola, Gruppo Friulano per una Nuova Fotografia and Il Ponte. He has published many photographs in the world of fashion and advertising, as well as on architecture, and has made countless reportages. Mainly in association with the Touring Club of Italy, he has produced books on Italy and other European countries. His wide-ranging œuvre has made him one of the most important postwar Italian photographers.
Gianni Berengo Gardin. Fotografie 1953–90 (Udine: Art&, 1990)
Lo studio di Giorgio Morandi (Milan, Florence: Charta, 1993)

Berlau, Ruth
(b. 1906, d. 1974) Denmark
Berlau cycled to Paris in the late 1920s and to Moscow in 1930, recording her adventures in a popular Danish daily newspaper. She became an actress and committed communist and founded the first workers' theatre in Denmark. After meeting Bertolt Brecht in 1935 she left her family and emigrated with him to Sweden, Finland, the USA, Switzerland and Berlin (1948). Berlau was one of Brecht's main literary collaborators. She used her Leica to reproduce manuscripts for duplication and recorded not only the development of stage productions but also Brecht's numerous meetings with other personalities of his time.
Hans Bunge (ed.) *Brechts Lai-Tu. Erinnerungen und Notate von Ruth Berlau* (Darmstadt: Luchterhand, 1985)

Bezzola, Leonardo
(b. 1929) Switzerland
Bezzola attended Otto Morach's art classes at the Zurich Kunstgewerbeschule (1949–50). During the 1950s he worked for large printing and reproduction companies and experimented with lithography, murals, photography and film-making. As a photographer he went on to concentrate on tourism, architecture, industry and, in particular, on collaborating with artists and writers. He has produced a large number of catalogues and art books with Bernhard Luginbühl, Jean Tinguely, Peter Bichsel and many others.
Jean Tinguely and Niki de Saint-Phalle. *Stravinskybrunnen Paris* (Bern: Benteli, 1983)
clic 2 (Zurich: Verlag Ernst Scheidegger, 1992)
Kunstaustellungen Holderbank (Holderbank Management und Beratung AG, 1994)

Bischof, Werner
(b. 1916, d. 1954) Switzerland
After attending Hans Finsler's photography classes at the Zurich Kunstgewerbeschule (1932–36), Bischof began working in fashion and advertising but after his military service (1939–45) he turned to reportage and travelled in Germany, France and Holland with Emil Schulthess for a special issue of *du*. During his travels through Austria, Italy, Greece and Eastern Europe, his central theme was the face of human suffering. Bischof worked in England, published in *Picture Post*, *Illustrated* and the *Observer* and became a member of Magnum in 1949. In 1951 *Life* magazine published a feature on famine in India that made him famous. In 1951 he became co-founder of the Kollegium Schweizerischer Photographen together with Gotthard Schuh, Paul Senn, Jakob Tuggener and Walter Läubli. His work in the Far East was shown in an exhibition in Zurich in 1953 and in another special issue of *du*. On an assignment to Peru and Chile in 1954 for Magnum and *Life*, Bischof was killed returning from the Inca town of Machu Picchu.
Japan (Zurich: Manesse, 1954)
Unterwegs (Zurich: Manesse, 1957)
Marco Bischof. *Werner Bischof. Leben und Werk 1916–1954* (Bern: Benteli, 1990)

Bisson, Auguste-Rosalie
(b. 1826, d. 1900) France
Auguste Bisson was the younger of the two sons of a heraldic painter. The brothers began experimenting with photography shortly after the daguerrotype came into use in 1839. Between 1849 and 1851 they produced 900 daguerrotype portraits of the members of the Assemblée Nationale, which were then lithographed. Subsequently the Bisson brothers turned to the reproduction of paintings and to documenting historic buildings and classical sculpture in France, Italy and Germany. In 1861 Auguste Bisson climbed Mont Blanc with a guide and 25 porters and, using a large-format plate camera, took not only the stunning panoramas of the Alps that made him famous, but also charted their arduous climb. The popularity of the Bissons' high-quality images diminished with the rapid spread of the small *carte de visite* format, as a result of which their joint studio went bankrupt in 1863.
Französische Photographie 1840–1871 (exhibition catalogue Kunsthaus Zurich, 1987)

Brancusi, Constantin
(b. 1876 Romania, d. 1957) France
Brancusi went to study sculpture at the Bucharest Academy of Art (1898–1902). In 1903–04 he travelled on foot to Paris, where he continued his studies at the Academy there. He met Auguste Rodin, and, declining Rodin's offer to work with him, he went on to become one of the most important modern sculptors. Inspired by Steichen, Stieglitz and later Man Ray, Brancusi took photographs of the work at his studio and developed an intense interest in self-portraits. In 1937 he travelled to India and to Romania, his home country, where he erected his *Endless Column* as part of a military monument. In 1954 his work was exhibited in Zurich in the exhibition *Begründer der modernen Plastik* (Founders of modern sculpture). Brancusi began to photograph under the guidance of Man Ray as early as 1905. Some of his 2000 photographs were first exhibited in Zurich in 1976.
Constantin Brancusi. Der Künstler als Fotograf seiner Skulptur (exhibition catalogue Kunsthaus Zurich, 1976)
Brancusi Photographe (Paris: Centre Pompidou, 1982)

Brandt, Bill
(b. 1904 Germany, d. 1983) England
Brandt spent his youth in northern Germany. At sixteen he contracted tuberculosis and spent seven years being treated in Davos, Switzerland. In Vienna, he was introduced to a circle through which he later met Man Ray in Paris. In 1929 he spent several months in Ray's studio, but without receiving formal instruction. He studied Surrealist art and films and met the Hungarian photographer Brassaï. In about 1931 Brandt finally settled in London and began to observe the social life of England in the 1930s. This led to two important books, *The English at Home* (1936) and *A Night in London* (1938). In addition to working as a journalist for publications such as the *Weekly Illustrated*, *Picture Post* and *Lilliput*, Brandt's freelance portraits, sombre landscapes and his book *Perspective of Nudes* (London 1961) had a decisive influence on the younger generation of photographers.
Mark Haworth-Booth (intro.) *Bill Brandt: London in the Thirties* (London: Gordon Fraser, 1983)
Ian Jeffrey (intro.) *Bill Brandt. Photographs 1928–1983* (London: Thames and Hudson, 1993)

Brassaï (Gyula Halász)
(b. 1899 Hungary, d. 1984) France
The son of a professor of French literature, Brassaï studied painting at the Budapest Academy of Art (1917–19). In 1920 he went to Berlin where he met Moholy-Nagy, Kandinsky and Kokoschka and obtained his diploma at the Hochschule für Bildende Kunst. In 1924 he moved to Paris, working as a painter and journalist, and soon made contact with the artistic avant-garde. He spent years observing and photographing the nightlife of Paris and in 1933 he published his sombre and intimate book *Paris de Nuit*, a milestone in the history of the photographic book. Brassaï also worked for a series of magazines and produced portraits of artists such as Bonnard, Braque, Giacometti and Picasso. His photographs for *Le Minotaure* brought him into contact with all the major Surrealists. Picasso inspired him to photograph the graffiti on the walls of Parisian houses. These photographs, which have an affinity with the Abstract Expressionist movement in

vogue in America at the time, were exhibited at the New York Museum of Modern Art in 1956.
Paris de Nuit. Nächtliches Paris (Munich: Schirmer/Mosel, 1979)
Brassaï (Paris: Centre National de la Photographie, 1987)

Brunner, Ernst
(b. 1901, d. 1979) Switzerland
After attending interior design classes at the Kunstgewerbeschule in Zurich, Brunner worked as an architect's draughtsman in Lucerne. He became unemployed in 1936 and began to photograph in an objective style. Between 1936 and the early 1960s Brunner recorded the rural life and traditional crafts of Switzerland in over 40,000 photographs. He then devoted himself entirely to the study of farmhouses and published *Die Bauernhäuser im Kanton Luzern* in 1977. Peter Pfrunder. *Ernst Brunner – Photographien 1937–1962* (Zurich: Offizin, 1995)

Burri, René
(b. 1933) Switzerland
Burri attended Hans Finsler's photography classes at the Kunstgewerbeschule in Zurich (1950–53). After working as a camera assistant, he managed to break into photography in 1955 with a report in *Life* on the musical training of deaf-mute children. Subsequently he photographed in the crisis areas of the Middle East, South America and, from the early 1960s, in the Far East, Africa and the United States. His photographs have appeared in all the major magazines, such as *Epoca, Life, Look, Paris-Match, Stern* and special issues of *du*, such as 'El Gaucho' (1959), 'Japan bei der Arbeit' (1961), 'In Deutschland' (1962), 'Tagebuch aus Polen' (1990) and 'Los Cubanos' (1993). Over a period of many years Burri has recorded political and social changes in various countries emphasizing the life of ordinary people. He is interested in civilizing influences, as reflected in his portraits of great artists (Picasso, Giacometti, Tinguely and many others), and the ruins left behind by war. Since 1959 Burri has been a member of Magnum and in 1982 he and Bruno Barbey organized the exhibition *Terre de Guerre* at the Magnum gallery in Paris.
René Burri.One World (Bern: Benteli, 1984)
Beyrouth (Paris: Editions des Cyprès, 1992)

Capa, Robert (André Friedmann)
(b. 1913 Hungary, d. 1954) America
After leaving school Capa decided to become a journalist. He began to photograph in 1930 with a Leica, but had to leave Hungary because of his political activities. He studied at the Deutsche Hochschule für Politik in Berlin and worked for the Dephot agency (1931–33). When Hitler came to power Capa moved to Paris and worked freelance for the Vu agency, *Regards, Ce Soir, Life, Time* and the *Weekly Illustrated* in London. As well as Henri Cartier-Bresson and David Seymour, he met the journalist and photographer Gerda Taró, who became his colleague and companion. From 1936 he sent regular reports on the Spanish Civil War and the Japanese invasion of China (1938). Taró died in Spain in 1937 and in 1939 Capa emigrated to the United States. At the end of the Second World War he accompanied the first American soldiers during the invasion of Normandy and his photographs were shown all over the world. In 1947, Capa joined Cartier-Bresson, Seymour and George Rodger as a co-founder of the Magnum agency. Capa travelled to Russia with John Steinbeck and reported from Israel from 1948 to 1950. He was killed by a landmine during the war in Indochina while taking photographs for *Life*.
Robert Capa: cuadernos de guerra en España (1936–1939) (Valencia: Salla Parpallo/IVEI, 1987)
Robert Capa (Paris: Centre National de la Photographie, 1988)

Carmi, Lisetta
(b. 1924) Italy
Carmi became a self-taught photographer from 1951, and turned professional in 1960. Carmi has published books of photographs of Israel (Milan 1965) and of Ezra Pound (New York 1968). In 1968 she began a study of transvestites. After several visits to India and meeting the guru Master Babaji she gave up photography in the late 1970s and devoted herself entirely to a spiritual life.
Ezra Pound (Munich: Kindler, 1978)
Fotografi Italiani: diario immaginario di Lafranco Colombo (Bologna: Edizione Bolis, 1993)

Carrieri, Mario
(b. 1932) Italy
Carrieri specialized in colour photographs of paintings to finance his freelance photographic work. This led to a large-scale personal portrait of his home town Milan, which appeared in 1960 as a book entitled *Milano, Italia*. Later Carrieri devoted himself exclusively to film.
Milano, Italia (Milan, Lerici, 1960)

Cartier-Bresson, Henri
(b. 1908) France
Cartier-Bresson studied painting against his father's wishes under André Lhote (1927–28). In 1932, after a year in the Ivory Coast and travels through Europe, he began to work as a photographer. He was in close contact with the Surrealists working on the periodical *Le Minotaure* and had his first publication and exhibition in 1933 (Julian Levy, New York). He accompanied an ethnographical expedition to Mexico (1934–35) and then turned to film, working with Paul Strand and as an assistant to Jean Renoir. A prisoner of war in Germany (1940–43), he escaped to Paris where he worked as a photographer in the underground movement. He then began a long series of portraits of artists. He worked in America (1946–47) and founded Magnum with Robert Capa, David Seymour and George Rodger. From 1948 to 1952 Cartier-Bresson lived and worked in the Far East. In 1952 he published his book *Images à la sauvette* in which he presented his philosophy of 'the decisive moment' in photography. Thanks to this book and his countless photo-reportages, which not only appeared in all the leading magazines but were also seen by a wide public in exhibitions and books, Cartier-Bresson was more responsible than any other postwar photographer for setting new standards in the art of high-quality photojournalism. Since the mid-1970s he has resumed his interest in drawing and painting.
Henri Cartier-Bresson (Paris: Centre National de la Photographie, 1982)
Henri Cartier-Bresson. Photoportraits (Thames and Hudson, 1985)
Peter Galassi. *Henri Cartier-Bresson. The Early Work* (New York: Museum of Modern Art, 1987)

Cerati, Carla
(b. 1926) Italy
Cerati began her professional career in theatre photography; she soon undertook reportage and began to take portraits of a wide variety of people. Her work on young people, intellectuals and those on the fringes of society has been published in a number of magazines such as *Illustrazione Italiana, Vie nuove* and *L'Espresso*. She produced a series on conditions in Italian mental hospitals, which was published in 1968 under the title *Morire di classe*. She is concerned with showing how the mentally ill have less chance of improving their situation when forcibly interned.
Morire di classe – La condizione manicomiale (Turin: Einaudi, 1968)

Cohen, Joan Lebold
(b. 1932) America
Cohen is an art historian and photographer who has lectured since 1973 at the Tufts University/School of the Museum of Fine Arts, Boston; she is currently Research Fellow at Harvard University's Fairbank Center for East Asian Studies. Cohen has visited Asia regularly since 1961 and spent over a year in the People's Republic of China (1979–80). There she gained a unique insight into the artistic and cultural life of modern-day China. As an author and photographer she has published a large number of books and essays on the new Chinese painting.
The New Chinese Painting 1949–86 (New York: Abrams, 1987)
Yunnan School. A Renaissance in Chinese Painting (Minneapolis: Fingerhut, 1988)

Dalain, Yvan
(b. 1927) Switzerland
Dalain studied at the School of Photography in Vevey (1946–49) and began his career as a freelance photojournalist. Until the 1960s Dalain produced pictures on France, Greece, Italy, Africa and Israel for *Die Woche, Collier's, Picture Post, Epoca, Paris-Match, National Geographic* and many others. Dalain is keenly interested in human reportage; he describes himself as a 'voleur d'âmes' (stealer of souls). Since 1960 he has become increasingly interested in advertising and has become a producer and director for Swiss television.
Les Petits des Hommes (Lausanne: La Guilde de Livre, 1954)
Vie et Mort d'un Toro Brave (Paris: Editions Denoël, 1964)

Davidson, Bruce
(b. 1933) America
Davidson studied photography at Rochester Institute of Technology (1951–54) and continued his training under Herbert Matter, Alexey Brodovitch and Josef Albers at Yale University. He worked freelance for *Life* between 1955 and 1957. In 1959 he became a member of Magnum and his photographs, mainly of New York, appeared in *Réalités, Esquire, Queen, Look, Vogue* and *du*. He was awarded a scholarship by the Simon Guggenheim Foundation in 1962, and in 1962 he exhibited works including his photographs of the Brooklyn gang called 'The Jokers' in the Museum of Modern Art. Davidson recorded life on East 100th Street in Harlem in New York with a large-format camera (1966–68) and *du* devoted an entire issue to these photographs, which appeared in book form in 1970. He turned to filming in the 1970s; between 1980 and 1982 he produced a series of colour photographs of the New York subway.
East 100th Street (Cambridge: Harvard University Press, 1970)
Bruce Davidson (Paris: Centre National de la Photographie, 1984)
Subway (New York: Aperture, 1986)

Davis, Greg
(b. 1948) America
Born in Los Angeles, Davis went to Vietnam as a GI in 1967. He has worked with *Time* magazine's team of photographers since 1989. He lives in Tokyo. Apart from long-term projects on the environmental destruction caused by reckless industrialization and on the collapse of the Chinese empire, Davis mainly photographs political and social changes in Korea, Cambodia, Vietnam and Laos.

Dübi-Müller, Gertrud
(b. 1888, d. 1980) Switzerland
Between 1904 and 1907 Dübi-Müller studied painting under Cuno Amiet. In 1905 she took her first photographs as visual mementos. She began to collect art in 1907 and was in close contact with painters, musicians and literary figures throughout her life, many of whom she photographed. She was a very close friend of Ferdinand Hodler from 1909 until his death in 1918. During that period Hodler painted a number of portraits of her, while she documented his late creative period in more than a hundred photographs.
Gertrud Dübi-Müller. Dokumentarphotographien (Solothurn: Vogt-Schild, 1984)

Fels, Florent
(b. 1891, d. 1977) France
Journalist, art critic, amateur photographer and a friend of Jean Cocteau, Fels published magazines such as *L'art vivant* and *Voilà* as well as albums of photography.
Hans Jürgen Syberberg (intro.) *Fotografie der 30er Jahre* (Munich: Schirmer/Mosel, 1977)

Ferrato, Donna
(b. 1949) America
Ferrato has worked as a freelance photographer since 1976. Her subject is violence in the family, on which she has published a book, *Living with the Enemy* (New York: Aperture, 1991). She lives and works in New York, where she is active on behalf of abused women.

Finsler, Hans
(b. 1891 Germany, d. 1972) Switzerland
After studying architecture and art history, Finsler worked as a librarian and lecturer at the Halle Kunstgewerbeschule (1922–32). A self-taught photographer, in 1926 he set up a special photography course. His first exhibition, *Neue Wege der Fotografie* (1928), attracted much attention, and like Moholy-Nagy and Renger-Patzsch, Finsler became a pioneer of the New Photography. In 1932 he was appointed to the Zurich Kunstgewerbeschule where where he set up a photography course which he taught until 1957. As a champion of the Neue Sachlichkeit or 'New Objectivity' he had a decisive influence on several generations of Swiss photographers.

Mein Weg zur Fotografie (Zurich: Pendo, 1991)
Staatliche Galerie Moritzburg Halle (ed.) *Hans Finsler Neue Wege in der Photographie* (Edition Leipzig/Bern: Benteli, 1991)

Frank, Robert
(b. 1924 Switzerland) America
Frank trained as a photographer in Zurich and gained his first professional experience in Geneva and Basel (1941–46). In 1947 he left Switzerland for Paris and Amsterdam, and then found work in New York in the *Harper's Bazaar* studio. He photographed in Peru and Bolivia (1948) and in the years that followed he tried to establish himself as a freelance photographer with projects on, among others, Spanish bullfighters and Welsh miners. A grant from the Guggenheim Foundation enabled him to photograph during several months of travelling across America (1955–56). Frank's photographs, showing a sombre America remote from the main highways, appeared as a book two years later in Paris, and in 1959 in New York. Initially savaged by the critics, *The Americans* became a cult book and Frank's subjective style became an influential model for many photographers. Working in the circle of Jack Kerouac and Allen Ginsberg, the exponents of the beat generation, Frank then began a long series of experimental and mostly autobiographical films.
The Lines of My Hand (Zurich: Parkett/Der Alltag, 1989)
Moving Out (Washington: National Gallery of Art/Zurich: Scalo, 1994)
Black and White and Things (Washington: National Gallery of Art/Zurich: Scalo, 1994)

Freund, Gisèle
(b. 1912 Germany) France
Freund studied sociology and art history in Germany (1931–33) and, after fleeing from the Nazis, at the Sorbonne in Paris. She began to take photographs for a living and published a report on the underprivileged areas of northern England in *Life*. She met André Malraux and began a series of portraits of writers and artists such as Sartre, Duchamp, Joyce and Shaw. Freund obtained her doctorate in 1936 with a sociological and aesthetic study of portrait photography in 19th-century France. During the war she fled to the south of France and then lived in Argentina until 1950. She published pictures of Indians in Tierra del Fuego, tin mines in the Andes and Evita Perón. After some years spent in Mexico she published a book on Ancient Mexico, before finally settling in Paris in 1954, where she returned to portrait photography.
Photographie und Gesellschaft (Hamburg: Rowohlt, 1979)
Gisèle Freund. Portraits von Schriftstellern und Künstlern (Munich: Schirmer/Mosel, 1990)

Garduño, Flor
(b. 1957 Mexico) Switzerland
Garduño studied visual arts at the San Carlos National Art School in Mexico City (1976–78). As assistant to Manuel Alvarez-Bravo, she collaborated with him on three portfolios of platinum and palladium prints (1978–80). As a freelance photographer, she produced art reproductions and published three books herself (1980–86). Garduño then worked for four years on the book *Witnesses of Time*, which was also shown as a travelling exhibition.
Bestiarium (Zurich: U. Bär, 1987)
Witnesses of Time (London: Thames and Hudson, 1992)
Mesteños (Frauenfeld: Schellenberger, 1994)

Geiser, Karl
(b. 1898, d. 1957) Switzerland
Geiser was a sculptor who taught himself photography, probably in the early 1920s. He mainly took pictures of his models, from which he could work in their absence. More rarely, he took personal views of the plaster models at various stages of completion in the studio. Geiser's legacy of some six thousand photographs also includes freelance photographic works in which he deals in a poetic but unflinching manner with everyday subjects.
Bernische Stiftung für Fotografie, Film und Video (ed.) *Mit erweitertem Auge. 'Berner Künstler und die Fotografie'* (Bern: Benteli, 1986)

Gnant, Rob
(b. 1932) Switzerland
After his education in Lucerne (1947–50), Gnant became a trainee camera assistant in Basle in 1951. From 1954 he worked as a freelance photographer, and his pictures appeared mainly in *Die Woche* and the weekend supplement of the *Neue Zürcher Zeitung*. He also collaborated on eight documentary films by Alexander J. Seiler. Since 1975 Gnant has worked as a cameraman in a film collective which produces films of political and social criticism. Recently he has concentrated on PR photography for business reports.
J'aime le cirque (Lausanne: Rencontres, 1962)
Made in Switzerland (Zurich: Vetter, 1977)

Griffiths, Philip Jones
(b. 1936) Britain
Griffiths studied pharmacy in Liverpool and practised in London. From the 1950s he also worked as a photographer, first for the *Manchester Guardian*, and then the London *Observer*. As a freelance photojournalist he has reported on the war in Algeria, on Central Africa, Asia and in particular on the Vietnam war, which led to his deeply moving book *Vietnam Inc.* In 1971 Griffiths became a member of Magnum; he photographed in the Yom Kippur War before being assigned to Cambodia and Thailand. He has produced a growing number of documentary films (most recently *A Welsh Eye*, 1991). He has lived in New York since 1980 and continues to treat subjects such as Buddhism in Cambodia, drought in India and poverty in Texas.
Vietnam Inc. (New York: Collier Books, 1971)
Bangkok (Amsterdam: Time-Life, 1979)
Dog Odyssey (London: Aperture, 1996)

Griss, Yvonne
(b. 1957) Switzerland
Griss studied industrial photography (1975–78). She specialized in photography at the Zurich Schule für Gestaltung (1978–80), and worked as a photographer at the Zurich Museum für Gestaltung (1984–87). Since 1986 she has published work in *du*, the *Tages-Anzeiger*, *Der Alltag* and other Swiss periodicals. As a freelance photographer Griss studies human behaviour.
Paul Hugger. *Fastnacht in Zurich. Das Fest der anderen* (Zurich: Orell Füssli, 1983)

Haas, Ernst
(b. 1921, d. 1986) Austria
After studying medicine at the beginning of the Second World War, Haas enrolled on the photography course at the Vienna Graphische Lehr- und Versuchanstalt (1943–44). He made a study of Vienna after the war and exhibited his photographs of Austrian veterans returning from the war at the Red Cross headquarters in 1947. These same photographs also appeared in *Heute* and *Life*. He worked as a freelance photojournalist in Paris and New York (1948–50), and in 1950 he became a member of Magnum, moved to the United States and spent the following years working for *Paris-Match*, *Esquire* and many other publications. His book *The Creation*, which tries to recapture the biblical story of the creation in colourful, sometimes abstract photographs, appeared in 1971.
Ernst Haas. *Die grossen Fotografen* (Munich: Christian, 1984)
Ernst Haas. *Farbfotografien* (Munich: Schirmer/Mosel, 1989)

Hahn, Walter
(b. 1889, d. 1969) Germany
Originally a lithographer, Hahn began to photograph during climbing expeditions in about 1910. He made his name with his photographs of landscapes and buildings in the so-called Saxon Switzerland (Germany) and Dresden. In the summer of 1943 he captured the famous splendour of the city of Dresden from the air. A year and a half later he personally experienced the bombing of the city and photographed the scene of total destruction from the tower of the town hall.

Hamaya, Hiroshi
(b. 1915) Japan
Hamaya began to photograph in 1931, and worked in a laboratory for a few years. In 1936 he published pictures of the Tokyo slums and became a freelance photojournalist. From the mid-1950s he worked on a series of picture stories on Japan, some of which appeared as books: *Snow Land* (1956), *Japan's Back Coast* (1957) and *Landscapes of Japan* (1964). Hamaya usually roams his home country on foot in order to experience nature intensely and to try to understand the local people and their customs. He has also worked in China, the United States and Australia and is regarded in Japan as one of the pioneers of photojournalism.
Hiroshi Hamaya: Fifty Years of Photography (Tokyo, 1981)
Landscapes (New York: Abrams, 1987)
Watashi (Shonan Bunko, 1991)

Haya, Maria Eugenia
(b. 1944) Cuba
Haya lives in Havana and works as a photographer. She is closely involved in building up the city's photography collection.

Herron, Matt
(b. 1931) America
Herron trained as a photographer at the Rochester Institute of Technology and became a private pupil of Minor White in 1957. Since 1962 he has been a freelance photographer and author for international periodicals. In 1964 he founded the 'Southern Documentary Project' with the help of Dorothea Lange to document rural life and social changes in the southern states of America at the beginning of the civil rights movement. During the 1970s Herron took photographs for Greenpeace to protest at Russian whaling. He was president of the American Society of Media Photographers (1992–95).
The Voyage of Aquarius (E. P. Dutton, 1974)
The Quilt: Stories from the Names Project (Pocket Books, 1988)

Hesse, Martin
(b. 1911 Germany, d. 1968) Switzerland
After training with an architect in Thun, Hesse studied at the Bauhaus in Dessau in 1932 and began to take photographs. He settled in Bern and soon worked mainly as a photographer. He produced reports on rural and urban daily life and documentaries which were commissioned for an inventory of the artistic monuments of the canton of Bern. He produced portraits of many Swiss artists and of his father, the writer Hermann Hesse, who lived in southern Switzerland from 1919.
Luc Mojon (intro.) *Album* (Langnau: Emmentaler Druck AG, 1987)

Hinz, Hans
(b. 1919 Germany) Switzerland
Hinz trained as a gravure-retoucher (1927–31). After his first self-taught attempts to produce three-colour photographs on paper in 1934, he produced his first publication in 1935. After further training as a photo-lithographer, he did pioneering work from 1941 as a colour photographer in his own studio in Basel. His interest in art and advertising brought him work for large European firms and publishers. Many of his colour prints appeared in *du* (1942–60). Hinz took photographs for over one hundred books, which include *Der Isenheimer Altar* (1939), *Die Schweizer Uhr* (1945), *Lascaux* (1955), *L'art populaire à Bali* (1976) and, most recently, *Glasmalerei des 16.und 20. Jahrhunderts im Basler Rathaus* (1994).

Hoyningen-Huene, George
(b. 1900 Russia, d. 1968) America
After the 1917 October revolution, Hoyningen-Huene fled with his mother from St Petersburg to England; he settled in Paris in 1921. He worked as a fashion sketcher and trained as a painter in André Lhote's studio. He collaborated with Man Ray and produced his first fashion photographs in the mid-1920s, and became fashion photographer for *Vogue*. He spent a year in New York and took portraits in Hollywood for Condé Nast (1929). In 1935 he moved to New York and was a fashion photographer for *Harper's Bazaar* until 1945. He then moved to Hollywood and taught at the Art Center School. In addition to his fashion photographs, which appeared in all the leading fashion magazines until the 1950s, he published books on classical Greece and Egypt in 1943.
The Photographic Art of George Hoyningen-Huene (London, Thames and Hudson, 1986)
Eye for Elegance, George Hoyningen-Huene (New York: Congreve Publishing Company, 1980)

Hunstein, Don
(b. 1928) America
Hunstein takes portraits of musicians for CBS.

Imsand, Jean Pascal
(b. 1960, d. 1994) Switzerland
After studying at the Basel Kunstgewerbeschule (1977–79).
Imsand studied lithography (1979–84). From 1985 he worked
as a freelance photographer in Freiburg, then in Zurich from
1988. He experimented with photomontages and portraits of
artists. Until his death he worked on a long-term study of
the difficult circumstances of life in the Zurich drugs scene,
in a home for mentally handicapped young people, in the
municipal soup kitchen and in Brocki-Land.
Vision (Zurich: U. Bär, 1992)
Urs Stahel (ed.) *Aus der Romandie* (exhibition catalogue,
Fotomuseum Winterthur, 1993)

Joya, Mario García
(b. 1938, d. 1991) Cuba
Joya worked in Cuba as a photographer and cameraman.
He exhibited throughout the world.

Kern, Thomas
(b. 1965) Switzerland
Kern has worked as a freelance photographer since
completing his training. He has reported from England,
Northern Ireland and Switzerland (1988–89), and has
also worked on documentary films. A co-founder of
the Lookat Photos agency in Zurich (1990), Kern has
regularly been commissioned by the *Tages-Anzeiger
Magazin*, *du* and *Stern*, in former Yugoslavia, Iraqi
Kurdistan, the Lebanon, Egypt and Northern Ireland.
Since 1994 he has taught photojournalism at the Zurich
Schule für Gestaltung.

Kertész, André
(b. 1894 Hungary, d. 1985) America
After studying at the Budapest business school, Kertész
began working at the stock exchange. He bought a camera
in 1913 and took photographs during the First World War.
In 1925 he settled in Paris and worked for *The Times* in
London, the *Berliner Illustrierte*, Vu agency and magazines
throughout Europe. He met Man Ray and André Breton's
circle of Surrealists. Under their influence Kertész created
his famous series of distorted photographs of nudes. He
captured the atmosphere of Paris life in the 1920s and
produced portraits of all his artist friends, who included
Brancusi, Mondrian and Tzara. He lived in New York
from 1936, published his book *Day of Paris* in 1945 and
worked for, among others, *Harper's Bazaar*, *Vogue* and
Look until 1949. He was contract photographer for *Condé
Nast* from 1949 to 1962. His Parisian work was rediscovered
in the late 1960s.
André Kertész. Sixty Years of Photography 1912–1972
(London: Thames and Hudson, 1972)
Sandra S. Phillips (et al.) *André Kertész. Of Paris and
New York* (Thames and Hudson, 1985)

Kizny, Tomasz
(b. 1958) Poland
When military law was introduced in Poland in 1982, Kizny
became a co-founder of the independent photography agency
Dementi, which worked for the underground movement for
seven years, documenting strikes, demonstrations by the
Solidarity union and social protest in general and supplying
foreign media with pictures. Kizny is currently trying to make
the Gulag system in the former USSR known to a wider
public with exhibitions of his own work and photographs
from Soviet archives.

Klein, William
(b. 1928) America
Klein studied social sciences in New York until 1948, and
went on to the Sorbonne in Paris. He worked in Fernand
Léger's studio and created murals for architects in France
and Italy. His career as a photographer began in 1954. He
was a professional photographer for *Vogue* between 1955 and
1965. In 1956 he published *New York*, a book of expressive
pictures of the big city. This was followed by books on Rome
(1958), Moscow and Tokyo (both 1964). He belongs to the
'Subjective Photography' group. Since 1965 Klein has
concentrated on film work.
Close-Up (London: Thames and Hudson, 1989)
In and Out of Fashion (London: Jonathan Cape, 1994)

Kobayashi, Masanori
(b. 1949) Japan
After four years working for the Mainichi newspapers,
Kobayashi works freelance in Kyoto. He has worked for
the UN High Commission for Refugees since 1980.
*Is the Sun Responsible? – A Report from the East
African Borders* (Osaka Play-Guide Journal, 1981)
Refugees – Struggles without End (1986)
Refugee Children (Tokyo: Ohtsuki, 1994)

Kubota, Hiroji
(b. 1939) Japan
Kubota studied political science in Tokyo and in the US.
Hiroshi Hamaya awakened his interest in photography and
he began to work as a freelance photographer in 1966. He
returned to Japan in 1968 and in the late 1970s he began to
photograph in Korea and China. He joined Magnum in 1989.
Korean Mountains, Baegdusan and Gemugangsan
(Tokyo: Iwanami Shoten, 1988)
Chine: Photos de Hiroji Kubota (Paris: Ecole Nationale
Supérieure des Beaux-Arts, 1989)

Lang, Candid
(b. 1930) Switzerland
Lang studied photography under Richard Aschwanden in
Altdorf (1948–51). He worked with Leonard von Matt and
Otto Pfeifer and trained with Martin Hesse and Paul Senn.
He has reported for the agencies Comet Photo AG and
ATP Bilderdienst, and for *Die Woche*, *Schweizer Illustrierte*,
Tages-Anzeiger and *Blick*. While recuperating from an illness
in 1983 he fulfilled his dream of working with an old,
large-format wooden camera.
Silvio Mattioli (Zurich: ABC, 1975)
Rigi-Bahn (Zurich: Orell Füssli, 1984)

Lange, Dorothea
(b. 1895, d. 1965) America
Lange worked as an assistant at various photographic studios,
including that of Arnold Genthe (1912–17). After attending
the Clarence White School of Photography (1917–18), she
opened a portrait studio in San Francisco in 1919 and worked
as a freelance documentary photographer until 1934. In 1930
she photographed the effects of the great drought in the
American south-west and in 1933–34 she recorded strikes
and unemployment in San Francisco. She was the chief
photographer for the Farm Security Administration (FSA)
under Roy E. Stryker (1934–39). Her *Migrant Mother* (1936)
is the most widely published FSA photograph. From 1942
on she worked for other government offices and between
1954 and 1955 for *Life*. She worked freelance in Asia, South
America and the Middle East from the late 1950s.
An American Exodus – A Record of Human Erosion
(New York, 1975)
Dorothea Lange: A Photographer's Life (New York:
Farrar, Straus & Giroux, 1979)
Carl Fleischauer et al. (eds.) *Documenting America*
(Berkeley: University of California Press, 1988)

Larrain, Sergio
(b. 1932) Chile
Larrain studied at the universities of California and Michigan
(1949–53) before taking up photography. On his return to
Chile he published pictures in various Latin American
periodicals. From 1956 he was employed by the Brazilian
paper *O Cruzeiro*, travelling in Argentina, Paraguay, Chile
and Peru. He was a member of Magnum from 1961 to 1970.
Photographs by Larrain have also appeared in American
magazines such as *Fortune* and *Venture*.
La Casa en la Arena (Barcelona: Lumen, 1966)
Chili (Lausanne: Editions Rencontre, 1968)

Lerski, Helmar (Israel Schmuklerski)
(b. 1871 France, d. 1956) Switzerland
The son of a Polish-Jewish emigré, Lerski lived in Zurich
from about 1876. Having travelled to Africa, he moved to the
United States in 1893 where he worked first as an actor and
from 1910 as a photographer. He returned to Europe in 1915
and settled in Berlin. He worked in films until the late 1920s
before concentrating on portrait photography: his series of
close-up portraits, 'Köpfe des Alltags' (Portrait heads from
everyday life), appeared as a book in 1931. He lived in

Palestine from 1932, working on various films and the series
'Jüdische Köpfe' (Jewish heads). In 1931 he spent three
months on a photographic project on 'transformations made
with light', a series of 175 portraits of a man taken in different
lighting conditions. He returned to Switzerland in 1948.
Fotografische Sammlung Museum Folkwang (ed.), *Helmar
Lerski, Lichtbildner* (Essen: Museum Folkwang, 1982)
Andor Kraszna-Krausz (intro.) *Verwandlungen durch Licht*
(Freren: Luca, 1982)

Linke, Armin
(b. 1966) Italy
Linke lives and works as a photographer in Milan. Since 1987
he has portrayed figures from contemporary theatre, art,
literature, music and film. He has also worked in fashion
(for *Elle*, *Moda*, *Vanity Fair* and others) and industry.
Dell'arte nei volti (Milan: Motta Editore, 1994)

List, Herbert
(b. 1903 Germany, d. 1975)
After studying literature and history of art at Heidelberg
University (1921–23), List joined his father's coffee import
business in 1924, which he took over in 1929. He met the
photographer Andreas Feininger who encouraged him to
take up photography. His first still lifes were influenced by
Surrealism (1930). After giving up the import business, he
attempted to establish himself as a photographer in Paris and
London (1935–36). He travelled to Greece and Italy, working
on the book *Licht über Hellas* (Light over Hellas, 1953). He
later travelled to southern Europe, North Africa and the
Caribbean and began a long series of portrait photographs.
Herbert List. Portraits (Hamburg: Hofmann und Campe, 1977)
Herbert List. Fotografia metafisica (Munich: Schirmer/
Mosel, 1980)
Herbert List. Hellas (Munich: Schirmer/Mosel, 1993)

Luskacová, Markéta
(b. 1944 Czechoslovakia) England
Luskacová studied social sciences at the Charles University in
Prague with a paper on religious traditions in Slovakia (1967).
She went on to study photography at the Prague Academy of
Film and Art (1967–69). She worked as house photographer
for the 'Theatre on the Balustrade'. Since settling in London
she has worked as a freelance photographer making studies of
physically abused women (1976–77), street musicians (1978),
clowns (1986–87) and children in England (since 1984).
Pilgrims. Text by John Berger (Arts Council of Great
Britain, 1985)
Exhibition catalogue with texts by M. Holborn, D. Widgery
and C. Killip (London: Whitechapel Gallery, 1991)

Lyon, Danny
(b. 1942) America
Lyon studied history at the University of Chicago (1959–63).
He worked as a freelance photographer recording
demonstrations during the American civil rights movement
(1962–64). He belonged to the 'Chicago Outlaws' biker's
club (1965–66). From 1967 he worked as a freelance
photographer mainly in Latin America. In 1971 Lyon
published his book *Conversations with the Dead* in
collaboration with the inmates of the Ramsey penitentiary
in Texas. During the 1970s he mainly worked on films.
Pictures from the New World (Millerton, Aperture, 1981)

Maisel, Jay
(b. 1931) America
After training as a painter and designer, Maisel studied
photography at Yale University with Herbert Matter and
Alexey Brodovitch (1952–56). Since 1954 he has worked
freelance for advertising agencies and industrial firms.

Merisio, Pepi
(b. 1931) Italy
Merisio worked as a freelance press photographer for the
Touring Club Italiano and magazines such as *Paris-Match*,
Look, *Réalités*, *Stern* and in particular *Epoca* from 1960. He
published his first book on the sculptor Bodini (1964). He
recorded all the travels of Pope Paul VI and produced a large
number of private commissions for the Vatican (1964–78).
He has published many books on various regions of Italy.
Pepi Merisio. 'I grandi fotografi' (Milan: Fabbri, 1982)

Miller, Wayne F.
(b. 1918) America
Miller served in Edward Steichen's Naval Aviation Unit of the US Marines (1942–46). From 1946 he was a freelance photographer in Chicago; financed by two Guggenheim scholarships, he photographed the life of black Americans in the northern states of America. He taught photography at the Chicago Institute of Design (1948–49). Miller lived in California from 1949 and worked for *Life* until 1953. He was Steichen's assistant for *The Family of Man* exhibition (1953–55) and became a member of Magnum in 1958. He was involved with various environmental organizations from the 1960s and retired from active photography in 1977.
The World is Young (New York: The Ridge Press, 1958)

Mohdad, Samer
(b. 1964) Lebanon
Mohdad spent his childhood in Beirut, fleeing with his family to the hills with his family after the Israeli invasion in 1975. He fought in the Lebanese militia, but decided to leave the country at the age of 18 after being involved in an ambush. Having studied photography in Belgium he has worked for the Vu agency in Paris since 1989, sending reports from North Africa, Iraq, Yemen, Syria, the Lebanon, Switzerland and elsewhere. He has travelled in seven Arab Mediterranean countries for *du* (1990–94). He lives in Lausanne and works at the Musée de l'Elysée photography museum.
Les enfants, la guerre (Lausanne: Collection du Musée de l'Elysée, 1993)

Morath, Inge
(b. 1923 Austria) America
After studying at Berlin University in 1944, Morath worked freelance for the United States Information Service in Austria, and edited the periodical *Heute* (1946–49). She worked with Ernst Haas and took up photography. Moving to London in 1951, she studied photojournalism with Simon Guttman, the co-founder of the Dephot agency. She worked as assistant to Henri Cartier-Bresson from 1953 to 1954, and became a member of Magnum in 1955. Morath published her first book, *Guerre à la tristesse*, in 1956. In the late 1950s she travelled to the Middle East and North Africa; in 1965 she travelled to Russia, and published *In Russia* with a text by her husband Arthur Miller in 1967. She learned Chinese and since 1978 has visited China many times, publishing two books about it. Morath has also taken portraits of modern artists and writers such as Naum Gabo and Pablo Neruda.
Olga Carlisle. *Inge Morath.* 'Grosse Photographen unserer Zeit' (Lucerne: Bucher, 1975)
Salesman in Beijing (New York: Viking, 1984)
Inge Morath: Retratos de hombres y paisajes (Madrid: Sala de Exposiciones de Canal de Isabel II/Consejeria de Cultura, 1988)

Mulas, Ugo
(b. 1928 Italy, d. 1973)
Mulas gave up law and took evening classes at the Brera Academy of Art. He joined a circle of intellectuals and artists and became interested in photography. He made studies of the poor quarters, the station and the suburbs of Milan (1954–55). While he earned his living with fashion photography, advertising and reportage, his main interest lay in the art world. Until 1968 Mulas portrayed artists in Italy and documented the events of the Venice Biennale. In 1964, 1965 and 1967 he travelled to New York, where he produced exceptional documents on the contemporary art scene. From the mid-1960s Mulas turned increasingly to the theatre.
Hendel Teicher (intro.) *Ugo Mulas. Fotografo 1928–1973* (Musée Rath Geneva and Kunsthaus Zurich, 1984)

Munzig, Horst
(b. 1933) Germany
Munzig took up photography from 1949 after he had been given a small plastic camera following an illness. He was encouraged by Herbert List, who also put him in contact with *du* after his first major trip to Ireland in 1960. He worked with *Twen* and *Camera*, among others, from the mid-1960s.

Namuth, Hans
(b. 1917 Germany, d. 1990) America
Namuth left Germany in 1933 when Hitler came to power

and moved to Paris. He began his career as a photojournalist working for the Vu agency and *Life* magazine. He reported from the Spanish Civil War (1936–37). He served in the Foreign Legion (1939–40) before emigrating to the United States (1941) and serving in the American army (1943–45). After the war Namuth studied with Alexey Brodovitch and Joseph Breitenbach in New York and worked as a photojournalist for *Look*, *Fortune* and *Time*. In 1950 he met Jackson Pollock, about whom he made a documentary film (1951). He also made films on the artists Albers, Brancusi, Calder, de Kooning, Kahn and Matisse as well as photographic portraits of more than two hundred painters, sculptors and architects.
L'Atelier de Jackson Pollock (Paris: Macula, 1978)
Artists 1950–81. A Personal View (New York: Pace Gallery 1981)
The Voice and the Myth. American Masters (New York: Universe Books 1988)

Niesz, Anita
(b. 1925) Switzerland
Niesz trained at the Zurich Kunstgewerbeschule (1944–48). From 1949 she worked as a freelance photographer for the *Neue Zürcher Zeitung*, *du* and *Werk*. She undertook commissions for the Schweizerische Flüchtlingshilfe refugee centre, the Pestalozzi children's village, Pro Juventute and Pro Infirmis welfare agencies. She has made numerous journeys to France, Italy, Ireland and South Africa.
Pierre Zoelly (intro.) *Anita Niesz. Fotografien* (Bern: Benteli, 1989)

Oorthuys, Cas
(b. 1908 Netherlands, d. 1975)
Oorthuys began to photograph in 1930 while studying architecture at the Academy of Fine Arts in The Hague. During the 1930s she joined the worker-photographers and the anti-fascist Resistance. Oorthuys was one of the group of photographers who recorded life during the Nazi occupation of Holland from within the underground movement. Their pictures, for which they risked their lives, were shown after the war in an exhibition called *Die untergetauchte Kamera* (The submerged camera) and a selection was published in *du*. A book on the 1944–45 winter famine appeared in 1947. She later photographed in Indonesia, New Guinea and Africa.
Het Laatste Jaar 1944–1945 (Amsterdam: Contact, 1970)
Cas Oorthuys fotograaf 1908–1975 (Amsterdam, 1982)

Page, Tim
(b. 1944) England
Page arrived in Vietnam in 1965 and became a photographer for *UPI* and *Time-Life*. He survived severe war injuries and played a prominent role in Michael Herr's book *Dispatches*. On his return he found a temporary home with the 'beat generation' on the American west coast. On the tenth anniversary of the fall of Saigon in 1985 he returned to South-East Asia for the first time, and he has since visited regularly.
Tim Page's Nam (London: Thames and Hudson, 1983)
Mid-term Report (London: Thames and Hudson, 1995)
Derailed in Uncle Ho's Victory Garden (New York: Touchstone/Simon and Schuster, 1995)

Pino, Giuseppe
(b. 1940) Italy
Trained as a photographer in Milan (1963–64), Pino worked as a freelance photographer and photojournalist from 1965. He was chief editor of the weekly magazine *Panorama* (1967–73). He has taken many portraits of artists.

Preisig, Dölf
(b. 1940) Switzerland
Preisig trained as a photographer (1956–61) and continued his photography studies at the Zurich Kunstgewerbeschule (1961–64). Since then, he has worked as a photo-reporter specializing in sport and aviatics. Since 1976 he has been chief photographer for the *Schweizer Illustrierte*.
Im Cockpit für die Schweiz (Zofingen: Ringier, 1989)
100 Jahre Bobsport (Zofingen: Ringier, 1990)
Dölf Preisig. Fotoreporter (Bern: Benteli, 1995)

Rau-Häring, Nelly
(b. 1947) Switzerland
After practical training with the Basel photographer

H. Höflinger (1964–65), Rau-Häring specialized in photography at the Lette-Verein in Berlin (1965–67). She worked for a press agency, then in advertising, and from 1980 as a freelance photographer. She observes people in the street with an unusual eye for detail and for the different atmospheres of day and night. She has travelled in the Far East, the Soviet Union, the United States and Turkey (1991).
Lichtungen. '66 Fotografien der Nacht' (Nördlingen: Greno, 1987)
Menschen in Berlin (Frankfurt: Eichborn, 1987)

Realini, Luigi
(b. 1925–1986) Switzerland
Realini worked chiefly as a printer from 1949 to 1982. A self-taught photographer, his work appeared in various daily newspapers.
Huldigungen an das Zeitungspapier (Basel: own publication, 1982)
Photographien von Luigi Realini (Basel: Graphische Betriebe Coop, 1983)

Riboud, Marc
(b. 1923) France
Riboud began to take photographs with his father's camera in 1937. He fought with the French Resistance (1943–44). He studied at the Ecole Centrale in Lyon (1945–48) and worked as an engineer until 1951, when he became a full-time photographer. His first published work, pictures of the Eiffel Tower, appeared in *Life* magazine (1953). A member of Magnum from 1955, Riboud travelled to the Far East, sending his first picture report from China (1957). Further reports followed from the Soviet Union, Africa, North and South Vietnam, Bangladesh and Cambodia. His pictures focus on human interest and are exhibited and published worldwide.
Marc Riboud: Photographs at Home and Abroad (New York: Abrams, 1988)
Marc Riboud (Paris: Centre National de la Photographie, 1989)

Roberts, Bruce
(b. 1930) America
Roberts has worked as a photographer in the southern states of the USA since 1955. Until 1961 he worked for the *Charlotte Observer* before going freelance. He has taken photographs for various books on North Carolina and, since 1966, for *Southern Living* magazine.
Plantation Homes of the James River (University of North Carolina Press, 1989)
American Country Stores (Old Seabrook, Conn.: Globe Pequot Press)

Rodger, George
(b. 1908, d. 1995) England
Rodger studied art at St Bees College in Cumbria. He joined the Royal Navy in 1927, and began to photograph on his journeys round the world. He lived in the United States from 1929 to 1936, and survived the Great Depression by doing casual work. He worked as a professional photographer for the BBC in London (1936–38), and as freelance photographer for the Black Star agency from 1939. He photographed the German air raids on London and became war photographer for *Life* magazine. Until 1945 he produced reports from all the theatres of war in North Africa, the Far East and Europe. He published the books *Desert Journey* and *Red Moon Rising* (1943). In 1947 Rodger swore never to take war photographs again. He co-founded Magnum with Robert Capa, Henri Cartier-Bresson and David Seymour. Rodger travelled across Africa from Capetown to Cairo (1948–50) and returned to Africa more than a dozen times over the following years, publishing a book on the Nubas in 1955. His reportages have appeared in *Life* and every international magazine of note.
George Rodger: Magnum Opus. 'Fifty Years in Photojournalism' (Berlin: Dirk Nischen, 1987)
Humanity and Inhumanity: The Photographic Journey of George Rodger (London: Phaidon, 1994)

Roiter, Fulvio
(b. 1926) Italy
Roiter studied chemistry in Venice (1946–49). He became a member of the La Gondola photographers' group (1949) and worked as a freelance photographer from 1953. He published the first in a long series of illustrated books on Italian cities

and landscapes in 1954. He travelled to America and the Middle East from 1957. He recorded the prehistoric inscriptions and drawings of Valcamonica (1963–65). He has published books on Brazil, Africa, Turkey and Mexico.
Fulvio Roiter. Photograph (Lausanne: Payot, 1981)
Karneval in Venedig (Lausanne: Payot, 1981)
Fulvio Roiter. 'I grandi fotografi' (Milan: Fabbri, 1982)

Saint-Paul, René
(b. 1908, d. 1992) France
Saint-Paul began his career with the Trampus agency (1930). After military service (1939–42), he worked as a reporter for *Le Matin* (1942–45), then for *Combat* with Albert Camus, André Malraux and others until 1974. Subsequently he worked for *Le Quotidien de Paris* and *Le Figaro Littéraire.*

Salomon, Erich
(b. 1886, d. 1944) Germany
Salomon studied engineering and zoology in Berlin, then jurisprudence in Munich and Berlin (1906–14), obtaining his doctorate. Between 1919 and 1926 he held a variety of jobs. He went on to work in the advertising department of the Ullstein publishing house and began to take photographs with a borrowed camera (1926–28). His sensational pictures of a murder trial, taken with a hidden camera and published in the *Berliner Illustrierte*, began his career as 'roi des indiscrets' (king of indiscretion), observing events in the Reichstag, in the Geneva Palace of the League of Nations and at the political summits of the early 1930s. His book *Berühmte Zeitgenossen in unbewachten Augenblicken* (Famous people in unguarded moments) appeared in 1931. His way of photographing secretly, using whatever light is available, lends his pictures great credibility. When Hitler came to power Salomon fled to Holland; he also worked in Britain and America for *Life* and the *Daily Telegraph* as well as Dutch periodicals. He was taken prisoner in 1943 and died with his family in Auschwitz in 1944.
Salomon. Portrait einer Epoche (Berlin: Ullstein, 1963)
Erich Salomon (Millerton: Aperture, 1978)

Sander, August
(b. 1876, d. 1964) Germany
Sander studied photography in Trier (1897–99). After travelling to Berlin, Magdeburg, Halle, Leipzig and Dresden (1899–1901), he took over a photography studio in Linz in 1902. In 1910 Sander moved to Cologne where he established his own studio, and began to photograph farmers in the Westerwald. After the First World War he met the artists' group the 'Kölner Progressive'. He embarked on a study of different human types, to be published as an ordered picture of society in 45 sections. The preview to this compendium of portraits of 20th-century man, the book *Antlitz der Zeit* (Face of the time), appeared in 1929 but was ordered to be withdrawn from sale in 1934 by the Nazis. Sander then turned increasingly to nature and landscape photography. He published collections of photographs on various regions of Germany (1933–37). A large number from over 40,000 of his negatives were destroyed shortly after the war.
Ulrich Keller. *Menschen des 20. Jahrhunderts* (Munich: Schirmer/Mosel, 1980)
Antlitz der Zeit (Munich: Schirmer/Mosel, 1990)

Scheidegger, Ernst
(b. 1923) Switzerland
Scheidegger specialized in photography at the Zurich Kunstgewerbeschule under Hans Finsler and Alfred Willimann (1945–48). He was assistant to Max Bill and worked in Werner Bischof's studio (1948–49). His first reportage on Italian approved schools appeared in the *Schweizer Illustrierte* in 1949. He was exhibition designer for the Marshall Plan in Paris (1949–52), where he had close contact with the art scene. He travelled widely, to the Middle and Far East as a freelance photojournalist for *Life, Picture Post, Paris-Match, Stern* and many others (1952–55). He was lecturer in visual arts at the Hochschule für Gestaltung in Ulm (1956–57). From 1958 he produced various books and films about his close friend Giacometti. He was picture editor of the weekend supplement of the *Neue Zürcher Zeitung* (1960–88). In the early 1980s he worked as a freelance film director for Swiss television, producing documentary films on the photo-reporter Hans Staub (1984) and other artists.

Alberto Giacometti – Von Photographen gesehen (exhibition catalogue Kunsthaus Zurich, 1986)
Ernst Scheidegger (Bern: Benteli, 1992)

Schmid, Henri
(b. 1924) Switzerland
Schmid trained as a lithographer and graphic artist. In 1948 he set up his studio in Zurich. He earned his living and financed his work as a painter with photographs and reportage. In 1949 he was awarded a Swiss art scholarship which enabled him and the photographer Peter W. Häberlin to travel to North Africa and through the Sahara. He moved his studio to the Cité des Arts in Paris (1968–69).
Henri Schmid. Ölbilder und Aquarelle (exhibition catalogue Kunstmuseum Winterthur, 1988)

Schuh, Gotthard
(b. 1897, d. 1969) Switzerland
Schuh worked as a painter after the First World War, with his first solo art exhibition in Munich in 1922. He returned to Switzerland in 1926 and began to take photographs in 1927. He became a member of the Basel painter's group 'Rot-Blau' in 1930 and exhibited with them. In Paris in 1932 he met Picasso, Léger and Braque. From 1933 he worked for the *Zürcher Illustrierte* and for the Vu agency, *Paris-Match* and *Life.* He was sent on assignment to England in 1937 by the *Berliner Illustrierte*, then went to the coal-mining area of Charleroi (Belgium) and to cover Mussolini's visit to Berlin. He travelled to Sumatra, Java and Bali from 1938 to 1939. His best-known book, *Inseln der Götter* (Islands of the Gods, 1941), ran into several editions. Schuh became picture editor of the *Neue Zürcher Zeitung* (1941–1960). During the 1940s he travelled to Italy and the South of France. He co-founded the Kollegium Schweizerischer Photographen with Werner Bischof, Paul Senn, Jakob Tuggener and Walter Läubli (1951). He published two more books, *Italien* (1953) and *Begegnungen* (1956), before returning to painting in 1961.
Manuel Gasser (intro.) *Frühe Fotografien 1929–39* (Zurich: Arche, 1967)
David Streiff (intro.) *Gotthard Schuh. Photographien* (Bern: Benteli, 1982)
Bruno Haldner (intro.) *Ein Zeitbild 1930–1950* (Bern: Benteli, 1986)

Schulthess, Emil
(b. 1913, d. 1996) Switzerland
Schulthess trained as a graphic artist and took photography at the Zurich Kunstgewerbeschule (1928–32). After five years as a freelance graphic artist he joined the publishing company Conzett & Huber in 1937. From 1941 he was responsible for the graphic design of *du*, but later became a picture editor and photographer. He specialized in colour photographs of panoramas, which became famous worldwide. In 1953 *du* commissioned Schulthess to travel to the United States and his photographs were published in five special issues and as a book (1955). He has worked as a freelance photographer since 1957 and published books on Africa (1958, 1959), Antarctica (1960), Japan (1969), the Amazon (1962), China (1966) and the Soviet Union (1971). In the 1970s Schulthess led pioneering work in the field of panoramic aerial photography.
USA (Zurich: Manesse, 1955)
Swiss Panorama (Zurich: Artemis, 1982)
Landschaft der Urzeit (Zurich: Artemis 1988)

Schwartz, Daniel
(b. 1955) Switzerland
Schwartz specialized in photography at the Zurich Schule für Gestaltung (1977–80). He has worked as a freelance photographer and since 1989 has been a regular contributor to *du* as well as photographic advisor to the editor. He completed his first major work in Greece between 1980 and 1986, followed by a study of the Great Wall of China from 1987 to 1989. Since 1991 he has been working on a new book on Bangladesh, Burma, Cambodia and Vietnam.
Metamorphoses. Greek Photographs (London: Thames and Hudson, 1986)
The Great Wall of China (London: Thames and Hudson, 1990)
Le Corbusier – Villa Turque (Fondation Ebel, 1990)
Delta (London: Thames and Hudson, 1996)

Sellerio, Enzo
(b. 1924) Italy
After completing his law studies (1944) Sellerio gained experience as a journalist and decided to become a photographer in 1952. He published a special edition of photographs of his home town Palermo in 1961. He spent several months in the United States working freelance for *Vogue* and *Fortune* (1965–66). In the late 1960s he founded his own publishing house, specializing in books on literature, art and photography.
Persone (Florence: Passigli, 1990)
Enzo Sellerio fotografo e editore (Verona: World Action Project, 1991)

Senn, Paul
(b. 1901, d. 1953) Switzerland
Senn trained as a graphic artist in Bern (1917–21). He worked as a graphic artist and advertising consultant throughout Europe (1922–30). From 1930 he had his own graphic design studio in Bern. He was taken on in 1930 by Arnold Kübler as photo-reporter for the *Zürcher Illustrierte*, where he formed the core of the team of photographers together with Gotthard Schuh, Hans Staub and Ernst Mettler. He made numerous reports on everyday life in Switzerland and from abroad, including for the Red Cross during the Spanish Civil War (1937–39). During the Second World War, Senn was a war correspondent; he published his book *Bauer und Arbeiter* (Farmers and workers, 1943) with an introduction by Arnold Kübler. Senn's social critiques were published in photo-reportages with texts by Peter Surava in *Die Nation*. His book *Die unbekannte Schweiz* (Unknown Switzerland) on a home for poor and abandoned children in Valais was published in 1944. After 1945 he again reported for the Red Cross from the ruins of Europe. He worked for the *Schweizer Illustrierte* in the United States (1946). He co-founded the Kollegium Schweizerischer Photographen (1951) with Werner Bischof, Gotthard Schuh, Jakob Tuggener and Walter Läubli. In 1951 he also travelled to Mexico, returning in poor health.
Guido Magnaguagno (intro.) *Paul Senn. Photoreporter* (Bern: Benteli, 1981)
Martin Schaub (intro.) *Paul Senn. Bilder aus der Schweiz* (Lausanne: Collection de la Mémoire de l'Oeil, 1982)
Bruno Halder (intro.) *Ein Zeitbild 1930–1950* (Bern: Benteli, 1986)

Singh, Dayanita
(b. 1961) India
Singh studied photography for six years at the National Institute for Design in Ahmedabad. She then specialized in photojournalism at the International Center of Photography in New York. On her return to India she worked as a freelance photographer studying subjects including AIDS sufferers, child labour, street artists, the struggle for equal rights for women, prostitutes, eunuchs and street children. At present she is working in New Delhi documenting the social and economic conditions that influence family life in India.

Singh, Rahul
(b. 1940) India
Singh studied at St Steven's College at the University of Delhi and completed his studies in history at Cambridge University. Since 1964 he has worked as a photojournalist for various Indian and international periodicals, and as editor of the *Indian Express* and the Indian *Reader's Digest*. He is currently working on a book on the Punjab and Bombay.

Smith, W. Eugene
(b. 1918, d. 1978) America
After brief studies at Notre Dame University, Indiana, and the New York Institute of Photography, Smith began to work for *Newsweek* in 1937. He worked as war correspondent covering the South Pacific, where he was seriously injured. After the war he produced photo-essays for *Life* on subjects including a country doctor (1948), a Spanish village (1951) and Dr Albert Schweitzer (1954), which are still models of honesty, humanity and presentation. He left *Life* and became a member of Magnum (1957–59), before working as a freelance photographer in New York and Japan. In 1971 he moved to Japan to document the environmental pollution and its disastrous effects on the town of Minamata.

Minamata (New York: Holt, Rinehart and Winston, 1975)
W. Eugene Smith: Let Truth be the Prejudice: His Life and Photographs (New York: Aperture, 1985)

Soavi, Giorgio (1923) Italy
Soavi is a poet, writer, and amateur of art who lives and works in Milan.
Giacometti, La Ressemblance Impossible (Paris, 1991)
Il Quadro delle Patate (Guanda, 1994)

Spacek, Vladimir
(b. Czechoslovakia 1945) Switzerland
Spacek studied art history at Charles University in Prague, and was awarded a doctorate in 1977. He was granted political asylum in Switzerland after being forbidden to publish or exhibit his work. He has since lived in Zurich as a freelance artist and photographer and produces committed photo-essays on sociological subjects and large-format sequences of pictures on light, space and time. He has taught in Prague, Dortmund and Zurich. In 1991 he was appointed professor of freelance photography at the Johannes-Gutenberg University in Mainz.
Martin Heller and Urs Stahel (ed.) *Wichtige Bilder* (catalogue, Museum für Gestaltung, Zurich, 1990)
Vladimir Spacek (exhibition catalogue, Galerie der Hauptstadt Prague, 1994)

Staub, Christian
(b. 1918) Switzerland
Staub trained as a sculptor in Zug and studied painting in Paris (1938–40). He specialized in photography at the Zurich Kunstgewerbeschule under Hans Finsler (1940–44). His work first appeared in *du* (1943), and later in other Swiss magazines and for the American Three Lions agency. He worked as a freelance photojournalist in Vienna (1946–48) and for an advertising agency in Biel (1948–58). He has published books on the circus (1955) and the town of Biel (1957). He was lecturer in photography at the Hochschule für Gestaltung in Ulm (1958–63) and at the National Institute of Design in Ahmedabad in India (1963–66), then professor of photography at the universities of Washington and California (until 1988). He has also undertaken freelance architectural photography work.
Christian Staub. Fotografien (exhibition catalogue, Kunsthaus Zug, 1979)
A propos de Christian Staub (exhibition catalogue, Musée de l'Elysée Lausanne, 1981)

Staub, Hans
(b. 1894, d. 1990) Switzerland
After studying business and agriculture, Staub fought in the war from 1914 to 1918. He gave up sculpture for photography in 1920. He trained and worked as a photo-laboratory technician in Zurich, Tessin and St Moritz. While working as a photo-engraver in Zurich (1923–30), Staub wrote articles for specialist photographic magazines and became an enthusiastic supporter of the 'New Photography'. He was taken on by Arnold Kübler as the *Zürcher Illustrierte*'s first photo-reporter. His politically and socially committed reportages on unemployment and labour disputes and on everyday life in rural and urban Switzerland became the hallmark of this modern Swiss magazine. His work was forgotten until its rediscovery in the mid-1970s. A documentary film, *Hans Staub. Photo-reporter von Richard Dindo*, was made in 1978.
Guido Magnaguagno (intro.) *Hans Staub. Schweizer Alltag* (Bern: Benteli, 1984)
Bruno Haldner (intro.) *Ein Zeitbild 1930–1950* (Bern: Benteli 1986)

Steichen, Edward Jean
(b. 1879 Luxembourg, d. 1973) America
Steichen emigrated to America with his parents at the age of two. He trained as a lithographer (1894–98). Although he was first recognized as a photographer in 1899, he continued to see himself as a painter. He co-founded Photo-Secession with Alfred Stieglitz (1902) and became an exponent of painterly pictorialism in photography. He lived in Paris (1906–14) and supplied Stieglitz's '291' gallery and the magazine *Camera Work* with modern art (Rodin, Matisse, Picasso, et al.). During the First World War he directed the US Air Force photography service and shortly afterwards abandoned

painting. He began to work as chief photographer for Condé Nast Publications in 1923 and published a large number of fashion photographs and portraits of actors in *Vanity Fair* and *Vogue* until 1938. After the Second World War, during which he headed a group of marine photographers, he became director of the photography department of the New York Museum of Modern Art (1947–62). During that period he organized one of the most popular exhibitions of photographs ever, *The Family of Man* (1955).
Christopher Phillips. *Steichen at War* (New York, 1985)
Edward Steichen. A Life in Photography (New York, 1985)

Steiner, Albert
(b. 1877, d. 1965) Switzerland
Steiner trained as a photographer in Thun and under Fred Boissonnas in Geneva (1892–98). In 1909 he opened his own studio in St Moritz and made notable interpretations of the Engadin landscape. His photographs, published in many books including *Das Goldene Buch vom Engadin* (The golden book of Engadin, 1936), were distributed by a postcard publisher, and made his name as a photographer.
Beat Stutzer (ed.) *Du grosses stilles Leuchten*.
'Albert Steiner und die Bündner Landschaftsphotographie' (Zurich: Offizin, 1992)

Stock, Dennis
(b. 1928) America
Stock trained under Gion Mili (1947–51). He worked as a freelance photographer for *Life, Venture, Paris-Match, Geo* and others. He became a member of Magnum in 1954. He photographed James Dean over a period of two years for a book. Stock took portraits of jazz musicians (1957–60) and published *Plaisir du Jazz* in 1959. He works in Italy and Japan and has continued to produce books, for example on St Francis of Assisi (1981) and Provence (1988).
James Dean Revisited (Munich: Schirmer/Mosel, 1986)
Made in USA. Photographs 1951–1971 (Ostfildern: Cantz, 1995)

Studer, Walter
(b. 1918, d. 1986) Switzerland
Studer trained as a photographer in Speiz (1935–37). He reported from England, Germany, Poland and Italy for the Photopress agency (1941–47). From 1948 he worked as a freelance photographer in Bern. In the 1960s he turned increasingly to advertising and industry. In collaboration with his son he published reports in more than 140 issues of the Swiss Verkehrszentrale review *Schweiz-Suisse-Svizzera* (1974–85).
Das Emmental in den fünfziger Jahren (Zurich: Rentsch, 1983)
Paul Hugger. *Berner Oberländer Fotografen* (1995)

Tomatsu, Shomei
(b. 1930) Japan
Tomatsu completed his studies at the Aichi University Institute of Economics in 1954. He taught himself photography and worked for the Iwanami publishing house (1954–56). He became a founding member of the VIVO photographers' group in Tokyo. In 1961 he produced a shocking picture report on the after-effects of the nuclear explosion in Nagasaki (1966). His main interest remains the changes to Japanese society in a period of total industrialization.
Shomei Tomatsu. Japan 1952–1981 (Graz: Edition Camera Austria, 1985)

Tuggener, Jakob
(b. 1904, d. 1988) Switzerland
Tuggener trained as an engineering draughtsman (1919–23). Deeply impressed by German expressionist silent films, he began to work as a self-taught photographer in 1926. He studied at the Reimann Schule in Berlin (1930–31). On his return to Switzerland, Tuggener worked as a freelance photographer. In 1937 he began to make his own silent films. Besides recording everyday life in Switzerland, industry remained Tuggener's main subject until after the Second World War. In 1943 he published his book *Fabrik* (Factory), which depicts the problems of industrialization in wartime in expressive images and a cinematic style. He then became keenly interested in photographing masked balls and New Year balls, but never had a book published on the subject. He co-founded the Kollegium Schweizerischer Photographen

with Werner Bischof, Gotthard Schuh, Paul Senn and Walter Läubli (1951). Tuggener published books on Switzerland (e.g., *Zürcher Oberland*, 1956) and, as a follow-up to the Swiss regional exhibition, *Forum alpinum* (1965).
Jakob Tuggener. Fotografien 1930 bis heute (exhibition catalogue, Museum der Stadt Solothurn, 1978)

Van der Elsken, Ed
(b. 1925, d. 1990) Netherlands
Van der Elsken studied sculpture for a year at the Amsterdam school of applied arts in 1943. He worked for the underground movement and the Resistance against Nazi occupation (1944–45). After training as a cameraman (1945–47) he decided to become a photographer, taking his first street photographs between 1947 and 1950. He worked in the Pictorial Service laboratory in Paris, taking photographs and living a bohemian life on the streets and in the cafés of Paris (1950–54). He published his first book *Love on the Left Bank* in 1956. After returning to Amsterdam he photographed for *Vrij Nederland* and began to make films. He travelled to Africa and around the world (1959–60), but then devoted himself solely to filming until the publication of *Sweet Life* (1966). He then produced more documentary films and books, among others on the Far East, South America, Japan and Amsterdam. He recorded the last two years of his life when he was suffering from cancer in the film *Bye*.
Elsken: Japan 1959–60 (Tokyo: Libroport, 1987)
Once upon a Time (Amsterdam, 1991)

Vogt, Christian
(b. 1946) Switzerland
Vogt trained as a photographer in Basel and worked as an assistant in London and Munich. He has worked since 1969 as a freelance photographer with his own studio in Basel. His work has appeared in *Time, du, Camera, Playboy Photo* and elsewhere. His work includes portraits, nudes, formal studio photographs as well as news photographs and studies of former battlefields. In 1985 *du* commissioned work from him for a special issue on Basel.
Christian Vogt. Photographs (Geneva: RotoVision, 1980)
Katzenschattenhase (Basel: Weise, 1989)
Licht streift über dem Flügel (Neidhart & Schön, 1991)

Weiss, Sabine
(b. 1924) Switzerland
Weiss trained as a photographer under Paul Boissonnas in Geneva (1942–45). She has lived in Paris since 1946; until 1950 she was assistant to the fashion photographer W. Maywald. She has worked as a freelance photojournalist since 1949, taking photographs in Europe, North Africa, the Middle and Far East and the United States for such magazines as *Esquire, Vogue, Holiday, Life* and *Paris-Match*. She became a member of the Rapho agency in Paris and Photo-Researchers agency in New York in 1953. Weiss has worked as a fashion photographer for *Vogue* (1953–60) and also photographs children and life in the streets of Paris.
Les Marchés et Foires de Paris (Paris: ACE Ed., 1982)
Intimes convictions (Paris: Contrejour, 1989)

Widmer, Eduard
(b. 1932) Switzerland
After business school studies and training, Widmer worked as a post office official until 1959. At the same time he studied with the painter Aja Iskander Schmidlin. He specialized in photography at the Zurich Kunstgewerbeschule (1959–62). He worked as a photographer in the advertising studio of J. Müller-Brockmann (1962–64) and for the Swiss regional exhibition (1963–64). Since 1964 he has been a freelance photographer in the cultural and social field and also in the fields of architecture, advertising and specialist photography. He has made several journeys to Turkey, which led to his first book, *Osmanische Türkei* (1965). This was followed by books on Zurich (1971), Swiss castles (1976) and the blind (1983). He has returned increasingly to painting since the late 1980s.
Heureka (2 books for the Zurich exhibition, 1991)
Sinan (Tübingen: Wasmuth, 1993)